Even Better

Even Better

Easier Ways to a Happier Life

EMILY FLORENCE

Copyright © 2024 by Emily Florence

All rights reserved.

This book may not be reproduced or used in any manner without written permission of the copyright owner or publisher except for the use of quotations in a book review.

Some names and identifying details have been changed to protect the privacy of individuals.

Paperback ISBN: 978-0-9898253-5-1

Hardcover ISBN: 978-0-9898253-4-4

E-book ISBN: 978-0-9898253-6-8

Written by Emily Florence

Good Day Publishing
226 W. Ojai Avenue
Suite 101-404
Ojai, CA 93023

www.EmilyFlorence.com

*For my niece, Emery.
The world is yours, kiddo!*

*"Happiness is not something readymade.
It comes from your own actions."*
- Dalai Lama

Contents

Dear Reader		15
1.	Live Your Life for You	17
2.	Know You Are Worthy of Good Things	22
3.	Choose Happier	24
4.	Bend With Life	27
5.	Be Good to Yourself	29
6.	Surround Yourself With People Who Make You Feel Good	31
7.	Don't Stumble Over What's Behind You	33
8.	Be the Lighthouse	35
9.	Let Bad Thoughts Go	37
10.	Find Things to Appreciate (Even When it's Hard)	40
11.	Turn Your Day Around	43
12.	Check in With Yourself	46
13.	Take Time to Be Alone	48
14.	Love, and Let Yourself Be Loved	50

15.	Know You Deserve to Be Loved, Just as You Are	53
16.	Ride Your Moods, Own Your Emotions	55
17.	Trust That You Will Be OK	58
18.	Don't Stand on the Sidelines of Your Life	60
19.	Feed Your Passions	63
20.	Create Before You Consume	65
21.	Expect Great Things	66
22.	Keep Your Dreams Alive	68
23.	Understand Rejection Is Redirection	71
24.	Don't Settle for Love	74
25.	Enjoy Your Solo Time	76
26.	Be on the Same Page With People You Date	78
27.	Love the One You're With	81
28.	Have Your Own Life Outside of a Relationship	85
29.	Go Easy After a Breakup	88
30.	Travel Solo	91
31.	Savor the Sweetness of Doing Nothing	94
32.	Make Someone Smile	96
33.	Trust Your Intuition	98
34.	Be OK With People Not Liking You	100
35.	Be OK With Not Liking Everyone	102
36.	Make Space in Your Calendar	104
37.	Honor Your Life Seasons	106
38.	Practice Patience	109

39.	Take a Daily Moment of Joy	111
40.	Be True to Yourself	113
41.	Know How Much You Matter	116
42.	Remember, You Know What's Best for You	118
43.	Have a Healthy Relationship With Money	120
44.	Clear Out Your Clutter	122
45.	Spend Time in Nature	124
46.	Be Good to Mother Earth	126
47.	Re-Think Success	128
48.	Follow the Signs	133
49.	Believe You Can	138
50.	Start Your Day in a Positive Way	141
51.	Eliminate Life's Little Annoyances	144
52.	Tune Out Drama	146
53.	Love Yourself No Matter What	148
54.	Step Away From Self-Blame	151
55.	Be Proud of Yourself	153
56.	Set Intentions in Your Day	154
57.	Take Good Care of Your Health	157
58.	Prioritize Sleep	162
59.	Move Your Body and Exercise	164
60.	Be Kind to Your Mind and Meditate	165
61.	Laugh, a Lot	167
62.	Scroll Social Media With Care	168

63.	Put Down Your Phone	170
64.	Be a Better Listener	172
65.	Practice Affirmations	174
66.	Create Healthy Boundaries	179
67.	Try Not to Take Things Personally	183
68.	Schedule Your Day in a More Productive Way	185
69.	Ask for Help	188
70.	Try Something New	190
71.	Try Not to Compare Yourself to Others	191
72.	Be Happy for People	193
73.	Plant Good Seeds for Others	194
74.	Be Part of Something	196
75.	Grieve Your Losses	197
76.	Make Peace With Uncertainty	199
77.	Go Easy With Life Changes	201
78.	Choose Love Over Fear	203
79.	Let Life Surprise and Delight You	205
80.	Be Open to Life's Possibilities	208
81.	Slow Down and Savor the Moments	210
82.	Take Vacations	212
83.	Find Your Happy Place and Go There Often	214
84.	Release Your Worries	215
85.	Forgive and Move Forward	219
86.	Flip the Script on Your Life Stories	222

87.	Don't Be Afraid to Choose Again	224
88.	Remind Yourself, Tomorrow Is a New Day	227
89.	Let the Little Things Go	229
90.	Take Inventory of Your Life	231
91.	Love Yourself More	234
92.	Accept Compliments	236
93.	Highlight the Good	238
94.	Keep in Mind, We're All Going Through Something	240
95.	Stay Calm and Holiday On	242
96.	Keep Going, Keep Growing	245
97.	Treasure Your Friends and Family	247
98.	Always Be Ready to Celebrate	248
99.	Enjoy Your Life More	250
100.	Spread Joy	252
101.	Trust Something Even Better Is in Store	255
	Dear Reader	260
	Acknowledgements	263
	About Emily Florence	267

Dear Reader

Life is messy. It's not fair and it doesn't always go as planned. We all face dark days, hard times and grief so painful it brings us to our knees. This is part of the human experience – no one is exempt. You may not be able to control as much as you'd like in life, but you are not helpless or cursed. No matter where you are right now, or where you've been, you have the power to create a life that's even better.

You should know from the start that my life isn't perfect. I am not perfect. I haven't conquered all of my goals or dreams. I've fallen short, made mistakes, had my heart broken and witnessed my health crumble. I've let my emotions get the best of me, I've hurt people I never meant to and I've been betrayed by people I trusted. At times, I've felt sadness so deep I could hardly get out of bed, and I know all too well how debilitating anxiety and overwhelm can be.

Still, I know my life is blessed. I haven't cracked all the codes, but there are many truths I've learned so far. I've learned how to seek out the good and create more moments of true happiness and peace. I've learned that life isn't perfect and there will always be something that's out of our hands, but it's also full of possibilities, and we are all capable of experiencing more joy, love, calm and ease. I've learned there's so much we can do to feel better each day – no matter what's going on around us.

That's what this book is about.

Some of the life lessons you'll read in the following pages I learned through trial and error. Others were passed down to me from family and friends I'm lucky to have in my corner. Some lessons come from my studies, including a Bachelor of Arts degree in Cultural Anthropology, a Master of Arts degree in Broadcast Journalism and a Life, Life Purpose and Career Coaching Certification. Other tips, tools and nuggets of wisdom I learned from people I've known in my daily life or crossed paths with through travels, and teachings I've put into practice from authors and inspirational figures. While not everything in this book may be your cup of tea (so please feel free to take what speaks to you and leave the rest!), it is my promise that what you read will change your life for the better – if you let it.

If you've lost your way in the sea of noise that can be our modern world, I hope this book helps you find your way home to the person you truly are and connects you with the life you are meant to live.

Thank you for joining me. I'm happy you're here.
Emily

"The purpose of life is to know yourself,
love yourself, trust yourself and be yourself."
- Yogi Tea

1.
Live Your Life for You

A big challenge we all face in life is showing up in the world as our true selves. We are often so afraid of rejection and judgment that we don't fully own who we are and what we believe in. It's why many of us spend years, decades even, being someone we're really not. Then we wake up one day and find ourselves locked into careers, relationships and even personalities that aren't what we intended or what we actually want for our lives. It's like we're playing a part we didn't even realize we signed up for.

Why?

Sometimes it's to please others, or to fit in. We're human and we all want to be liked and accepted. Other times we simply don't know any better. We haven't questioned how we were raised, or what we've been taught to be right, wrong, good or bad. Sometimes fear of the unknown paralyzes us, and even though life as we know it isn't comfortable in a good sense, it's what we know, and we don't know what else we'd do.

Regardless of why, it's no way to go through life.

In an interview, a journalist once asked me, "What's the best decision you've made so far in your life, Emily?"

My answer came easy.

"Dropping out of law school after four days. I had no idea what I wanted to do with my life when I finished college and law school was something I applied for and got into, so I went. And even though I felt really cool saying, 'I'm going to law school,' by my third day I knew it wasn't something I wanted. And if I stayed, I'd only be doing so to prove to everyone that I could do it.

That was the moment in my life when I realized at the end of the day it didn't matter what people thought or said about me; what mattered was how I felt. In making the decision to leave, I chose to live my life for me."

Interviews are designed to get to the point, but there's more I want to say about leaving law school. It was by far the best decision I'd made in my life at the time, and not only because most likely I wouldn't be where I am today had I continued down that path, but it set a precedent for how I was going to move forward – making choices based on what would make me happy.

My third day of law school, I found myself staring out the classroom window thinking, "What have I gotten myself into?" We first-year law students had just been told that by the time we graduated our whole way of thinking would be changed, and nothing about that or anything we were learning excited me.

Class concluded and the guy sitting next to me asked me what I thought about our latest assignment.

"I don't really care," I said, surprising myself and my fellow student. "I don't think I belong here."

"Me neither!" He blurted and we peered over our shoulders to see if anyone had heard us.

And just like that it was crystal clear I'd be happier selling pretzels at a stand I passed by in the Boston Common on my way to school than to sit through another Torts class.

My heart knew I didn't belong in law school, but even with an unwavering voice inside saying, "This *isn't* for me," big decisions are rarely that simple. I sacrificed a great deal to get to where I was. I missed out on a whole lot of senior year of college fun and even Thanksgiving with my family cramming for the LSAT (the Law School Admission Test). I packed up my life and moved 3,000 miles across the country from my hometown of Ojai, California to Boston, Massachusetts. And I was happy in Boston. I loved the city. I'd made great friends, and the plan was to spend the next three years in school and then practice law. What would I do with my life now?

But law school was suffocating my soul. What I wanted for my life, or really, what I *didn't* want was clear, but the idea of my decision disappointing anyone and fears of what people would think about me made me ill.

I called my parents and asked how they'd feel if they ran into friends and neighbors and someone asked how I was doing in law school. Would my parents have to explain? Would they feel ashamed? I imagined conversations where my name would come up and people would say things like, "Ooh, did you hear Emily Florence dropped out of law school? She probably couldn't hack it." The best part of giving weight to these imaginary conversations was they were between people I hardly even knew, or liked!

Right then I realized how often in my life I'd done things for the approval of others, or because something was the popular or cool thing to do. Also, out of ego to appear successful or smart versus because it would make me genuinely happy. That's why dropping out of law school was such a paramount decision for me; I finally chose to prioritize how I felt on the inside over how I appeared on the outside.

As it turned out, I had all the support in the world from my parents, my brother and all of my family and friends – they just wanted me to be happy. That's all any of us want for the people we love when it comes down to it. While I did leave Boston for a while, a year later, I returned to do my Master's in Broadcast Journalism at Emerson College, which turned out to be such a better fit for me *and* I had the time of my life. And as for the naysayers and imaginary haters, it's a funny thing that happens when you own your life. Instead of being met with ridicule you're met with admiration. The best part? It doesn't matter to you either way.

> I finally chose to prioritize how I felt on the inside over how I appeared on the outside.

In the bestselling book, *The Top 5 Regrets of the Dying*, longtime hospice worker Bronnie Ware chronicled her patients top regrets in the last weeks, days and breaths of their lives. Do you want to know the number one regret so many of them had? They wished they'd had the courage to live their lives in a way that was true to who they were and what they really wanted, not the life others expected of them. As many of her patients said goodbye to this lifetime, they died with unfulfilled dreams and life goals knowing full well it was because of choices they did, or did not make.

It's not always easy to prioritize how you feel on the inside over what the outer world thinks or wants of you. We all crave acceptance and none of us want to let anyone down. But you don't want to one day look back on your life wondering what might have been had you only taken a chance on a dream, or found the courage to say "No, thank you" to something you knew in your heart wasn't right for you.

At the end of the day and at the end of life, you are left with you. Find the courage to live a life that's true to you.

2.
Know You Are Worthy of Good Things

We get the life we believe we deserve. While many of us want good things, we may not truly believe we deserve them. Whether it's the side of town we grew up in, the school we went to, our eating habits, or any past mistakes we're still punishing ourselves for, we often think we have to be different or better than we are right now in order to have a good life.

Thankfully, it's not true.

You are worthy and deserving of feeling happy, being loved, having great health, making money doing what you enjoy, traveling, smiling, laughing, loving – simply because you're alive. Whether you know it or not, you deserve to be, do and have everything you want.

Throughout life, people may tell you what you can or cannot do, or how something will play out for you. They may mean well, but keep in mind they're coming from their own perspectives and their experiences don't have to turn into your reality. Just because something in life happened one way for them doesn't mean it has to be that way for you, too. Like bestselling author Abraham Hicks says, "It may be true for them, but it doesn't mean it has to be true for you."

Starting now, forget what anyone has told you and ditch any beliefs holding you back. Believe in yourself like it's your number one job and know that you don't have to be or act differently in any way to deserve good things. You deserve the very best right now.

*"The most important thing is to enjoy your life
– to be happy – it's all that matters."*
- Audrey Hepburn

3.
Choose Happier

Life is precious, and it goes fast. It's all too easy to let the little disruptions or dramas take up our time and energy, and send us off purpose. That's why you have to wake up each day and deliberately choose more happiness.

We often think being happy depends on what our lives look like on the outside – the house, car, job, family, vacation, etc. Or when we reach a milestone or satisfy a condition, a.k.a. the "I'll be happy *when* …" syndrome. But happiness, in a large part, is an inside job.

Some people are naturally optimistic, while others struggle with mental, hormonal and other health issues that can make feeling good more of a challenge, and may need assistance from a doctor or specialist. Not every day will be sunshine and rainbows for anyone, but we all have the power to create more happiness when we choose it.

Throughout your day, be intentional to boost your joy levels and:

1. Seek out laughter and activities that make you feel good.
2. Limit bad news and drama.
3. Surround yourself with people who bring out the best in you. Let go of anyone who brings you down.
4. Entertain thoughts that make you feel excited and hopeful. Let go of ones that make you scared or upset. (With thousands of thoughts coming into our heads daily, it's impossible to filter them all. We can, though, recognize the ones we give our attention to for more than a few minutes and choose to let go of thoughts that make us feel bad.)
5. Take note of everything you have to be thankful for.
6. Choose books, podcasts, music and TV that make you laugh and feel inspired. Take a pass on entertainment that makes you angry, tense or has you sobbing into the couch pillows.
7. Take walks to clear your head and release feel-good endorphins, and choose food and beverages that make your body feel good. Be moderate with cocktails and heavy foods. (Let's face it, it's hard to be happy when you're bloated or hungover!)
8. Meditate. Even 10 minutes a day can change your life.
9. Be of service and lend a helping hand to a friend, neighbor or the planet.
10. Do at least one thing each day that brings a smile to your face.

This may sound silly or too good to be true, but when you decide you're going to be happier and you choose it throughout the day, these seemingly small things will add up to a significant amount of joy.

Not every day will be bliss, but each day brings a buffet of opportunities for you to feel even *a tiny bit* better. Remember, you are behind the steering wheel of your life. Be intentional and choose more of those things that make you feel good and less of anything that doesn't.

*"You can't stop the waves,
but you can learn to surf."*
- Jon Kabat-Zinn

4.
Bend With Life

The palm is one of the strongest trees in the world because it bends with the wind. Even when facing a hurricane, these resilient beauties know how to lean, so they come out standing tall once the storm passes. Unlike other trees that are rigid and inevitably break, the palm adapts, and so it survives.

There's so much we can't control in life – traffic, technology glitches, flight delays, people we love, people we don't, the neighbor's dog that's barking while you're trying to get lost in a good book. We can't control what's out of our hands, so the best thing we can do for ourselves when caught in the eye of a storm is to be like the palm tree and bend.

How we move with life is often our choice, and the more we push against what we can't control, without meaning to, the more we allow those things to break us.

Instead of exhausting yourself trying to control everything in life, seek to adapt. Make peace with what's out of your hands, have faith in the unknown and trust that everything will be OK.

The more you bend with life, the easier it is to ride out the storms.

5.
Be Good to Yourself

The most important relationship you will have in life is with the person staring back in the mirror. You are with you from beginning to end, in good times and bad, throughout your whole life journey. You owe it to yourself to be good to yourself.

We rarely mean to go down the self-criticism spiral, but often find ourselves there anyway. No matter how much we accomplish, we continue to put ourselves down and think we should be further along, better and more like someone else who we think is doing life the "right" way.

We push ourselves to the max from the moment we wake up until the time we hit the pillow at night and get down on ourselves when we fall short of crossing everything off our to-do list. But would you ever tell your best friends they weren't doing enough? Would you ever be so hard on them as you are on yourself?

It's easy to treat the people we care about with kindness and support. It's natural to see the best in them and encourage them to no end. When they're down, we assure them everything's going to be OK and remind them they're amazing and will bounce back. We don't scare or judge them. We pop Champagne to celebrate their wins, shower them with hugs when they're feeling low, and unconditionally love them. It's easy to do it for others, so why is it so hard to do it for ourselves?

Loving ourselves isn't optional. We teach people how to treat us by showing them the behavior we'll accept and not, and we have to have our own backs and be good to ourselves in order to expect others to be good to us, too. So instead of being hard on yourself, be supportive, compassionate and go easy.

None of us can be on all the time and there's always going to be more to do, so stop breaking your back each day trying to tackle it all and make everything perfect. Take off your overachiever hat and give yourself a rest from stress. Be OK with not going the extra mile and simply enjoy yourself for a change.

We all love giving our best, but we need time to relax and recharge to fully be our best. It's not lazy, it's loving.

6.
Surround Yourself With People Who Make You Feel Good

We all need quality people in our corner. Having friends and family you can laugh with and feel supported by is imperative to a happy life.

Sometimes though, we spend our time with people who don't exactly lift us up, have our backs, or make us feel all that good about ourselves, or life. It's quite easy, in fact, to get caught up with people who, when you think about it, you're not *really* a fan of.

You can't always choose who you hang out with (there are co-workers, neighbors, relatives or your kid's best friend's parents who you can't escape!). But there are also times when we find ourselves saying "yes" to people who we know deep down aren't that enjoyable to be around.

Other people's energy, even in small doses, can have a huge impact on our lives. That's why it's important to be aware of how the people you surround yourself with make you feel and if the feeling isn't all that good, give yourself permission to take a pass on invites or kindly excuse yourself early.

The world is full of wonderful people and your time and energy are precious. Filter out those people who don't make you feel all that great about yourself or life, and reserve yourself for the people who make you feel good.

7.
Don't Stumble Over What's Behind You

Years ago, my mom shared with me a Buddhist parable about two monks crossing a river. It goes something like this …

A senior monk and a junior monk were traveling together and came upon a wide river with a strong current. Nearby, a young woman also needed to cross the river and asked the monks if they would help her. The monks had taken vows never to touch a woman, but nonetheless, the senior monk picked the woman up and carried her across the river, gently placing her down on the other side.

The monks continued on their journey and the junior monk was visibly upset. For hours, he huffed and puffed until he couldn't contain himself anymore and blurted out, "As monks, we vowed not to touch a woman. How could you have carried that woman across the river?!"

The senior monk paused and looked at his junior and kindly said, "My brother, I set the woman down on the other side of the river hours ago. Why are you still carrying her?"

Our past is an important part of our history. It shapes who we are today, after all. But it can also be our biggest nemesis, one that's holding us back from growing into the person we truly want to be.

Many of us would like to rewrite parts of our past differently: opportunities missed, bad judgment calls in love, business, and life, disappointing people who we never wanted to hurt, and all those "shoulda, woulda, coulda's" that can come back to haunt us. Even though we can't undo what's been done, at times we still torture ourselves by living life looking back in the rearview mirror.

We can learn great lessons from our past mistakes, but often we look back on them far after the learning is done. And dwelling on what's behind you only keeps you from moving forward. **In order to step into a greater life, you need to stop looking back on the one you left behind.**

Next time you notice something from your past is interrupting your peaceful present or interfering with a brighter future, tell yourself, "I won't continue stumbling over what's behind me." Then turn your attention forward.

There's no need to keep living your life looking back in the rearview mirror. You don't live there anymore.

*"Don't forget that you may be
the lighthouse in someone's storm."*
- Unknown

8.
Be the Lighthouse

If you've ever been at sea in the middle of a pitch-black night and seen a lighthouse, you know it's more than an iconic structure to help boats navigate. To sailors, that bright light shining out of the dark is hope, comfort, and a source of joy.

There's so much negativity in this world and it's important to do what we can to look on the bright side and spread positivity.

Throughout your day, set an intention to make the world a better place and be aware of what you say and do. Keep in mind when you start a negative discussion with friends and family or post something online, someone else's mood will be impacted — and often in a bad way. Be mindful of what you are putting out into the world and ask yourself if it lines up with who you truly are, or who you want to be.

When a friend comes to you with a problem, be a beacon of hope and, when appropriate, help them discover silver linings. Give compliments to strangers and loved ones, share funny jokes, and tell one person each day how great they make your life. Be the first to smile, wave and wish people a good day.

We have so much more power than we may think to be a bright spot in the world and to make the people around us feel good. Spread joy with reckless abandon and when times are especially dark, remember to shine on like the lighthouse.

"Watch your thoughts, they become your words; watch your words, they become your actions; watch your actions, they become your habits; watch your habits, they become your character; watch your character, it becomes your destiny."
- Lao Tzu

9.
Let Bad Thoughts Go

"I can let this thought go."

I say this to myself daily. I'll be walking my dog Harper at the beach, so happy to watch her play in the soft golden sand and enjoying the gentle morning sun on my face and without warning, BAM, a bad thought pops into my head.

It could be something a politician said the day before that got under my skin or a comment a neighbor made that seemed like a compliment, but was it? Maybe a worry thought snuck in about something that may or *may not* happen down the road like, "What if I miss my flight next week, then what will I do?" Perhaps Harper and I crossed paths with someone earlier who wasn't all that friendly, and now, even though the person is far out of sight, I'm still replaying the encounter. It could even be something completely imaginary.

Thoughts can take you from happy to hopeless in a matter of minutes. They're that powerful. But with thousands of thoughts coming into our heads daily, it's impossible to filter them all. We can, though, control the ones we give our attention to for more than a few minutes and keep those from taking us out of the present and down a negative spiral.

If you're walking down the street, enjoying your day and suddenly find yourself thinking about something that makes you feel sad, mad, scared, worried or any other negative emotion, make the choice to tell yourself:

"I can let this thought go."

"I don't have to think about this right now."

"Don't even go there!"

Then fill your mind with something pleasing in front of you, something you're grateful for, looking forward to, or the most positive outcome of any situation you are facing.

It's important to note, not all negative thoughts should be pushed away. Uncomfortable thoughts deserve our attention when we're unpacking and processing something we're going through. After all, we're in the business of being happier for the long haul, not denying, repressing or putting a band-aid on life's hardships! It's beneficial, too, when you're coming up with creative solutions to a problem.

But as humans our memories run long and can be triggered quickly. Too often we keep alive something that we've already worked through, learned, healed and moved on from. Instead of falling back down a rabbit hole you've already emerged from, simply remind yourself to let that thought go.

Pay attention to the thoughts you give your attention to and as you go about your day, ask yourself, "Does thinking about this make me feel good?" When you realize you're stewing in something negative, replaying a bad memory or worrying about something you don't need to think about right now, then prioritize your happiness and let that thought go.

Like bestselling author Dan Millman said, "You don't have to control your thoughts. You just have to stop letting them control you."

"Be thankful for what you have; you'll end up having more. If you concentrate on what you don't have, you will never, ever have enough."
- Oprah Winfrey

10.
Find Things to Appreciate (Even When it's Hard)

In my late 20s, I discovered the power of gratitude and how it can completely transform your life. I was living in L.A. when I hit a low point and continued spiraling downwards. A little impatient and overly ambitious, I didn't "have" as much as I thought I would at that point and the feeling of coming up short consumed me.

For months, I struggled to get my first business off the ground. My apartment flooded from the above tenants' clogged toilet, and I was living on my friend's couch with the personal belongings that did make it through the flood locked in my car. Then my car broke down with the windows rolled down, leaving everything I owned exposed.

Even in our darkest moments we can always find something to be thankful for, but at this point it was feeling tough. For weeks, it seemed the worse things got, the worse things got.

One morning, I woke up exhausted from hearing myself talk and sick of the negative thoughts swirling in my head. I was like a broken record, repeating the same complaints over and over. I knew right then that something had to change. *I* had to change.

I decided to stop giving my energy and attention to the big things in my life that weren't going so great, and start focusing on the little things that were.

The perfect parking spot in front of the coffee shop.

The elderly gentlemen who held open the door for me at the post office.

The sweet text from an old friend that made me smile.

I bought a journal and decided at the end of each day to write down five things I was thankful for. (And when I say journal, I mean one of those yellow notepads from the grocery store – nothing fancy.) Not only would I write five things down, I decided, but I'd give each a few minutes of attention so I could feel in my body how appreciative I was for them.

Some days the five came pouring out and other days I sat stumped on number three, racking my brain to find *anything* else to be thankful for. But I stuck with it, and in only a week, I noticed positive shifts occurring in my life.

I slept soundly through the night.

I felt calmer and more peaceful in my body.

My mood improved and I rediscovered unexpected laughter.

Yes, my business still struggled. Yes, I was still without a home. But I wasn't as disappointed or bothered so much by what I *didn't* have. Life started feeling sweet again and in a short matter of time, the little daily things I was giving thanks for were joined by major life milestones.

Many people say practicing gratitude is the secret sauce for a happy life. All I know is the more I live in appreciation from sunrise to sunset, and feel in my bones how thankful I am, the more ease, joy and contentment I experience throughout my day.

> The more you seek to appreciate, the more you'll see to appreciate.

When life feels hard, or you're just trying to get by, it can be challenging to see all the good that's happening. Or worse, it can feel like there isn't any good! But even in the worst storms you can find things to be thankful for. Dig deep if you have to and give as many tokens of appreciation as you can, even if it's only for little things like that first sip of coffee, making a green light or feeling the sunshine on your face.

Take time each day to give thanks for all the good in your life and count your blessings big and small. The more you seek to appreciate, the more you'll see to appreciate.

*"Some people walk in the rain,
others just get wet."*
- Roger Miller

11.
Turn Your Day Around

No matter how intentional you are to have a carefree day, every so often you'll encounter grumpy people, common annoyances and stumbling blocks.

There's the driver who cuts you off and then has the audacity to yell at *you*. Or the software upgrade to your computer that you didn't want, don't know how to stop and now you can't do anything but scream!

We all have days that start out great, then something happens and we're pulled off track. But when your day takes an unexpected turn for the worst, remind yourself that you are in control of the wheel and follow these important steps:

Get it out

You're upset, and you probably have every right to be. It's healthy to get things out, so acknowledge your upsets, vent out loud to yourself or call up one person to vent to. Then, decide you're not going to allow any person or event to have that much power over you. Stop replaying what happened in your head or thinking about what you *could have* said or done differently, and instead decide to let it go. The sooner you drop it in your mind, the sooner your day will be back on track.

Make lemonade

When life hands you a lemon, ask yourself, "What good can come from this?" Your answer immediately shifts your thoughts to positivity and empowerment and away from feeling like a victim. When you seek out silver linings and intend to make the best out of any situation you feel strong and self-assured. Instead of feeling like something happened *to you*, you'll be able to see it as something that's happening *for you*.

> When life hands you a lemon, ask yourself, "What good can come from this?"

Counter negatives with positives

For every person or thing that gets on your nerves, give a few minutes of your attention to what's gone well in your day so far. Think of the person who said "hello" to you at the grocery store, the friend who sent a funny text, the sunny day *or* rainy day, and anything else standing out in your otherwise really good day.

Do something that will lift your mood

Take a walk and clear your head. Give your dog a belly rub. Read a few pages of an inspiring book or press play on a feel-good podcast. Do something that will boost your joy levels and make you feel even a *tiny bit* better.

An important way to prioritize our own happiness is by letting others' negativity roll off us. Don't let any person or annoyance get the best of your day, because they don't get to decide how you feel – you do.

"I restore myself when I'm alone."
- Marilyn Monroe

12.
Check in With Yourself

It's easy to lose touch with ourselves and lose sight of what we truly want in life. That's why it's important to schedule self-check-ins to connect with the real you, clarify your life intentions, and get excited for what lies ahead.

Every month or so, take a few minutes to savor a cup of coffee or sip a glass of something that makes you happy, and ask yourself:

How am I doing? *Really?*

How am I sleeping these days?

What's the first thing I think about in the morning?

What am I craving in life right now?

How do I start and end my days?

What could I use help with?

What's holding me back from feeling my best?

If I could vent to someone and just get everything out, what would I say?

Pay attention to what stands out. We often hold the answers to the questions we most seek, but we need time to slow down and be real with ourselves in order to hear them.

10 Signs it's time to connect with yourself

10. Lately you've been feeling … predictable. You're not sad, but you're not exactly *excited* about life.

9. "I'm fine with anything" is your go-to answer when someone asks you to choose a restaurant or movie to watch. Really, you *are* fine with anything. But then you think, "When was the last time I made an actual decision?"

8. You haven't had a really good laugh in ages.

7. It's been a while since you've fulfilled a dream or long-term goal. Even worse, you can't remember any dreams or goals! The future seems so blank.

6. Lately when you look in the mirror, you think something along the lines of "blah."

5. Your last journal entry was January 2nd.

4. "Things are crazy!" or "I need a drink!" has become your daily mantra.

3. Friends or family *may* have commented on how much you glance at your phone.

2. You're often on the brink of … crying, yelling, or hiding out in the bathroom!

1. Work, your relationships and life in general seem to be great, but something feels empty, like something inside is telling you, *I need a challenge* or *I need a new adventure.*

13.
Take Time to Be Alone

The word "alone" comes from *all oon*, meaning "all one."

It's not always easy to take time to be "all one" with ourselves, especially with busy work days, family and errands to run. But it's healthy to allow ourselves solo time and we often forget how much we truly need it.

Time alone isn't something to be rewarded with after trudging through a rough week. Me Time isn't earned, nor is it a luxury you should feel guilty about. It's necessary to slow down, reset and be "all one" with yourself.

Whether it's a few minutes alone in your car before walking in the door after work, an afternoon sipping lattes at a café with a good book, or an entire day holed up at home, take time for yourself. Schedule it in your calendar if you need.

It's impossible to be on all of the time and we all need timeouts to slow down, clear our minds and to recharge. So, give yourself permission to slip into a bubbly bath, take a long walk in nature, stretch out on a yoga mat or stare into a starry sky.

Take it easy and know that you deserve this sacred time.

> Me Time isn't earned, nor is it a luxury you should feel guilty about. It's necessary to slow down, reset and be "all one" with yourself.

*"There is only one happiness in this life,
to love and be loved."*
- George Sand

14.
Love, and Let Yourself Be Loved

My Aunt Bonnie passed away on the day I turned 30. I didn't particularly want the attention of turning 30 years old and my Aunt Bonnie never wanted attention for anything, especially dying, so it worked out for us both that we, in a way, shared the day.

"You two were that close," my mom and dad said of it.

My Aunt Bonnie was more than a typical aunt – she was my friend and my go-to for sharing my love life, or lack of it. She'd join me in excitement when a new man entered my life, squealing at every adorable detail, and, never failing, was there to nurse my wounds when disappointment hit. Aunt Bonnie would introduce me to everyone we crossed paths with as her favorite niece. Worth noting, I was also her *only* niece!

When I was young, Aunt Bonnie had married, but it didn't work out. Through the years there were a few suitors, but nothing seemed to last. She was so wonderful, I never understood why.

Shortly before Aunt Bonnie passed, when her illness was worsening by the day, I received a letter from her in the mail. Though I would visit her in just a few days for the hardest goodbye, she wanted me to have her parting words for me on paper. It was a few pages and rather personal of course, but there was one part I've always felt compelled to share when on the subject of love …

"Years ago, a friend asked me, what's another hurt? I feared the pain of love more than the pleasure. I learned too late that one must always allow herself to love and be loved. Always let yourself be loved, Emily."

I wanted to tell my Aunt Bonnie that it wasn't too late. I wanted to pick up the phone and call her up and say that she *could still* love and be loved. But the truth is, it was.

Love is everywhere. It's in every story and in the heart of every human being. We all want that kind of real love and partnership with someone who's your best friend and lover. A person who totally gets you, accepts and loves you, and has your back no matter what. But after disappointment hits, it can be easy to fear the pain of love or to simply be exhausted from all the drama and say, "I'm out!" (After all, once you've had food poisoning, the last thing you want to do is return to the restaurant.)

Some people say we never love the same after we've been hurt. That's the beauty of young, unjaded love. We have no reason to put up walls, guard our hearts, or ponder outcomes. We love at full capacity because we don't know that giving our hearts completely can be anything but awesome.

The path isn't always easy to this thing we call love, but it's a highlight of living. Even with no guarantees that it will last forever, do your best to let go of any past pain holding you back and go for it wholeheartedly. This time, every time. It's the only real way to live and the only way to love.

To be vulnerable to love is fantastically courageous.

15.
Know You Deserve to Be Loved, Just as You Are

I, along with people all over the world, fell in love with Mark Darcy the moment he told Bridget Jones he liked her very much, just as she was. As Bridget told her friends, "Not skinnier, or apart from the smoking, drinking, vulgar mother and verbal diarrhea."

He liked her just as she was.

Each and every one of us desires love and acceptance. We want to be with someone who likes us for all of our quirks, not despite them. And the thing we often forget is we deserve just that.

Whether you're dating for fun or looking for a long-term partner, you deserve to be with someone you can be 100% yourself with. There's no need to ever convince someone to love you, or to spend time with anyone who doesn't treat you in the amazing way you should be treated. Life is too short to walk on eggshells or feel insecure, and the best partners are not only the ones you can be yourself with, but who love you for it.

You don't have to be different in any way to be loved. You deserve to be loved right now – just as you are.

"The way I see it, if you want the rainbow, you gotta put up with the rain."
- Dolly Parton

16.
Ride Your Moods, Own Your Emotions

Life isn't 24/7 sunshine and rainbows. Lows happen to all of us. Sometimes there isn't even a reason we feel sad, anxious, angry or blah. Blame it on the moon, stars or waking up on the wrong side of the bed.

It's your birthright to experience emotions and it's important you allow them. (All of them!) They're not who you are, they are what you feel, so there's no need to judge yourself for them either. We're human and experiencing disappointment, heartbreak, frustration and all of life's lows is normal. In fact, even a growing number of doctors agree it's healthy to allow these emotions to surface rather than stuff them away.

Life can be so packed with to-dos that we don't always take time to connect with our feelings because there's somewhere we need to be or something more important to do. It's the "I don't have time to deal with this!" syndrome.

Since showing emotion makes us vulnerable and reveals our insecurities and imperfections, some of us simply won't allow ourselves to go there. God forbid we come off weak or irrational! But give yourself permission to feel all you do, free of self-judgment *and* keep in mind it's only a mood or season. This isn't the rest of your life. Negative feelings always eventually give way to better ones, so there's no need to make life-changing decisions or take drastic action when you're in a bad-feeling place.

There's a great poem by the philosopher Rumi called *The Guest House* that talks about inviting each emotion into your life like a guest into your home. He says, *"Welcome and entertain them all ... Even if they're a crowd of sorrows, who violently sweep your house empty of its furniture, still treat each guest honorably. He may be clearing you out for some new delight."*

> Give yourself permission to feel all you do, free of self-judgment **and** keep in mind it's only a mood or season. This isn't the rest of your life.

Get to know your emotions and take time to listen, learn and understand where they stem from. Talk with friends, therapists and coaches to unpack and process what's going on – it's healthy and cathartic. Just keep in mind the goal is to work through unwanted emotions so you can let them go and not throw gasoline on the fire. Because nothing good comes from stewing in *anything* negative for too long.

No matter how Zen you are, you'll most likely have moments where you overreact, forget to count to three and totally lose your shit! Just try not to take your bad mood out on others. No one deserves it and it can cause a negative ripple effect in the world.

Ride your moods and own your emotions. Welcome them like guests into your home and learn from them. Then, when the time is right, kindly bid them goodnight.

17.
Trust That You Will Be OK

When life has you down. When fear has such a strong hold on you that you are taking shallow breaths. When heartbreak has you blinded by tears, remember to breathe and tell yourself, "It's going to be OK. I am going to be OK."

You are strong, you are resilient, you've been through tough times before and you will get through this too.

You may feel like you are all alone in this moment or that no one understands what you're going through, but know that you are supported. No matter what you are experiencing, someone else is going through it right now, or already has, so reach out, connect and find comfort knowing you are not the only one.

When it seems like our lives are falling apart, we have to be real with ourselves and accept that it's healthy to feel. And we feel a whole lot when our wounds are raw.

This is a time to be extra good to yourself and:

Counter negative self-talk with kindness.

Talk with friends or connect with people in a support group.

Get a change of scenery and break with your usual routine for a day.

Listen to inspirational podcasts, read uplifting books and watch feel-good shows.

Take showers and put on real clothes – even if you don't feel like it.

Crack open the door to brighter possibilities by asking yourself, "What unexpected good can come from this?"

Make a plan for the future or a way forward that makes you feel better when you think about it.

Shine a spotlight on everything that's going well in your life and all that you *do* have to be thankful for.

This moment may be hard, but it isn't the rest of your life. Remind yourself, "I will get through this. I *am* getting through this. Everything is going to be OK."

Because it will.

*"The brave may not live forever –
but the cautious do not live at all."*
- Richard Branson

18.
Don't Stand on the Sidelines of Your Life

Have you heard the story about the man who prayed to God to win the lottery? Each day this man prayed, "God, please let me win the lottery. Please, God, please let me win the lottery." Finally after a year of praying, God answered him back: "My son, would you please go buy a ticket?!"

It makes sense; if we want something in life, we have to go for it. Yet, many of us are walking around with dreams we haven't even attempted to catch. We have endless reasons (or excuses) to keep us at length. It's too late in our lives, we don't have the time, it's too risky, it's better to stick with something we already know. But often, underneath lies another reason, a bigger reason – we're scared. After all, what if we struggle? What if we fail?

I'm not going to lie, going after a dream can be scary, and for me, setbacks have been part of the journey. My first book was rejected by publishing houses more times than my agent could keep track of – and there's nothing fun about waking up at 3 a.m. feeling like the bottom's about to drop out! But look around, and you'll see just how many people *do* experience what some would call "failure": Elvis, Walt Disney, Steven Spielberg, Thomas Edison, Michael Jordan, Emily Dickinson and Fred Astaire are just a few of the incredible people who at one point had been rejected, fired, or told they'd never make it.

Bestselling author Paulo Coelho said, "I ask myself: are defeats necessary? Well, necessary or not, they happen ... The secret of life, though, is to fall seven times and to get up eight times."

Things may not work out exactly as planned, but often in life something we initially consider a devastation, we later look back on as a gift from the universe, a blessing in disguise, because we wouldn't be where we are today had it played out otherwise. Hard-learned lessons, mistakes, time we feared lost, can be exactly what's needed to propel us into the next chapter of our lives. At the very least, disappointment and setbacks afford us the opportunity to witness our deepest strengths. They challenge us and when we rise back up (and we always do!) we see we're now stronger, wiser, more fearless versions of ourselves.

Having walked through hell and survived sets us free.

In a college acting class I learned that on the stage, no matter how good or bad one act goes, there will always be another to follow, and to go into each with courage and be prepared to adapt as needed.

Life is a series of acts, some go better than expected, and others don't. But it's not about playing it so safe that you never fail. It's about picking yourself up when you do and going into the next act with as much determination and enthusiasm as if it's the first.

You may think it would be easier to go through life playing it safe, but when something calls out to you, by whisper or blow horn, you have to find the courage to roll the dice.

If you're lucky enough to have a dream, something that no matter how hard you try or how many years pass by you can't shake, you owe it to yourself and the world to step off the sidelines of your life and go for it. It may be scary, but greatness comes from taking risks.

After all, the only way to score is by taking a shot.

"Don't ask what the world needs, ask what makes you come alive and go do that, because what the world needs is people who have come alive."
- Howard Thurman

19.
Feed Your Passions

Passion is what we're here to experience. It gives us a sense of purpose and makes us feel alive. When you engage your passions you give oxygen to your soul. You know you're living rather than merely existing and it takes you away from everything else.

We're all called to different things in life, but the feelings of passion we experience are universal. For you it may be writing, being in nature or around animals, traveling to new places, hiking, playing music, cooking, gardening, surfing, painting or working on creations with people who inspire you. Whatever it is, you know your passions because you're eager to do them and feel fulfilled when you're done. They make you lose track of time in the best way.

If you have the chance to make a living doing something you have passion for, do everything you can to make it happen. Since most of us will work for more than half of our lives, take small steps now to turn making a living doing something you love into a reality. These days, a job is rarely just a job anymore – it's a lifestyle. And we're not meant to feel anxiety on Sunday knowing the next day we have to be somewhere we don't truly want to be, working on things we don't really care about. We are meant to wake in the morning feeling eager for the day.

Whether you can do something you have passion for full-time, or not, make regular time in your schedule for those things that light your soul on fire. They keep you in harmony *and* keep you happy.

Passion fuels us. It makes you jump out of bed in the morning and give thanks for being alive. Feed your passions. Follow them. They bring life to living.

*"To change your life, you need
to change your priorities."*
- Mark Twain

20.
Create Before You Consume

It's easy to wake up and jump right onto your phone, scrolling the news or social media. But if you truly want to accomplish more of those things that matter to you, or be intentional to fulfill a life dream, you need to create something positive in your own life first.

What's one thing you could do that would make you feel better about your life? Change your diet and lifestyle for good? Read more books? Make better friends? Learn to dance the tango? Master cooking a new meal?

Start your day by prioritizing what's important to you, before getting led off track by other people's agendas. Be deliberate to move the needle in your own life and take action on those things that matter to you. Do you first – everything else can wait.

21.
Expect Great Things

As children, we believed we could do anything. There was no limit to what you knew you could accomplish, whether that was learning to walk, climb a tree or grow up to become an astronaut or president. You expected great things.

Fast-forward to adulting and many of us have gone from confident kids to Murphy's Law cynics gravitating toward the old adage, "Anything that can go wrong *will* go wrong." Instead of fully believing we can be, do or have something, our expectation of "when" it will happen has been replaced with "if."

If I get that promotion.

If we get to take that vacation.

If I can buy a house.

What we say and think has a bigger impact on our lives than we may understand. Though we don't mean for it, all of this "if-iness" can actually hold us back from those exact things that we want. We often think if we set the bar low we'll be pleasantly surprised, but the truth is when you expect great things, you're more likely to experience them.

What's one thing you want for your life right now? To open a restaurant, vacation in Spain, marry your person?

Try saying to yourself, "**If** _____ (this thing that you want) _____."
Now, say, "**When** _____ (this thing that you want) _____."
Feel the difference?
It's the same for when you say, "I hope to" or "I wish for" versus when you expect it.
Try saying to yourself, "**I hope to** _____ (insert your desire) _____."
Now, say, "**I expect to** _____ (insert your desire) _____."

When you say "**when**" and "**I expect**" you feel it stronger in your bones. It gives you a surge of confidence and your brain begins feeling like it's a done deal. It's like speaking something into existence – without even realizing it, you're setting things in motion.

Starting now, call on your inner child and approach each day with high hopes and positive expectations. Shake off past disappointments and begin expecting good things to happen in your life.

Like thoughts, words are powerful game changers, so be aware of what you say to yourself and to others. Think of your words like food for a garden; they'll either create a life that flourishes or one that flops.

Choose those words that help you grow.

"You'll see it when you believe it."
- Dr. Wayne Dyer

22.
Keep Your Dreams Alive

My brother Brent is one of my best friends and favorite people on the planet. Growing up, I adored my big brother and wanted to do all the things he did. I also deeply desired a little sister. "A big brother and a little sister. That will be the best!" I'd say to myself.

I asked my parents to make me a baby sister (having no idea what that meant). I made wishes on birthday candles and dandelions. I even asked Santa Claus and, one Christmas morning, he brought me a beautiful life-sized baby doll I named Megan. I treasured Megan and, in my little girl heart, I believed wholeheartedly that if I loved and cared for her enough, one day she'd turn into a real-life baby sister. All that hope temporarily went out the window the day one of my brother's mean friends yanked her from my arms and ran around the house squeezing her head and tormenting me to tears. And yet, when Megan was returned to my arms by my big brother, I kissed her forehead still believing there was a chance for a sister.

A few years later, my Aunt Mary gave birth to a beautiful baby girl, my cousin Jessa. My mom and I brought my aunt and cousin home from the hospital and when we opened the front door and faced the steep staircase to the nursery my aunt froze.

"I can't carry her up the stairs, it's too scary!" She said, handing my sleeping cousin over to my mom.

"What makes you think I can do it?!" My mom handed Jessa back to my aunt.

Back and forth these best of sisters went, debating who would carry my sweet cousin up the intimidating staircase. Finally, I stepped up.

"I'll do it!" I said and took my sleeping cousin into my arms and step by step climbed the staircase.

When I reached the top, I looked back to my relieved aunt and mom and down to my sleeping cousin. "I got you, baby girl," I told Jessa. And in that moment, I knew that all of my wishes, prayers and believing over the years had come true. My little sister was here.

Dreams can come true in ways you never expected. That's why it's important to keep your dreams alive. It's easy to get trapped by specifics, thinking that something has to happen in a specific way, by a specified time, or involving a specific person, or it's not going to happen. But anything really *is* possible in life, and there is always a way to reach those things you want when you remain open.

Life works in magical ways. Keep in mind it's not your job to know exactly *how* things will work out in your favor, but it is your job to keep believing they will.

> Life works in magical ways. Keep in mind it's not your job to know exactly **how** things will work out in your favor, but it is your job to keep believing they will.

23.
Understand Rejection Is Redirection

My senior year of high school, I spent a good three weeks by the mailbox waiting for a thick envelope to arrive from my top choice college welcoming me with open arms. I'll never forget the day I received a flimsy rejection letter instead.

I felt the same disappointing feeling in my stomach years later when a guy I was crazy about didn't feel the same for me, and a few years after that when a company I desperately wanted to work for went another way.

It would take years of feeling the sting of rejection before understanding that I was never being rejected at all. I was being redirected to something even better. Every. Single. Time.

We're only human, so when we don't get something that we have our heart set on, when something doesn't go as planned or someone doesn't feel the same way we do about them, it's natural to feel disappointed.

"What's wrong with me?" we may wonder. "Why not me?"

But what if every time we could know we're being redirected to something even better?

Whether it's a job, relationship, project, home or anything else that doesn't play out as planned, what if we simply said to ourselves, "Well, that just means something better is in store for me." And continue on our merry way.

What's funny about "rejection" is how often we don't *truly* want the job, school, house, club or person we feel rejected by. We have reservations deep down and often find ourselves letting out a sigh of relief, or eventually saying, "You know, I was never 100% sure about that. Thank goodness it didn't work out!"

A few months ago, a friend called me hysterical after being let go from her job. Did I mention my friend loathed her job? And for months she'd been saying how she wanted to work someplace else, but didn't have time to look for anything?

The same kind of phone call took place with another friend who had his heart broken by a man who, in truth, my friend had noted a handful of red flags about on date one.

Often, beneath the hurt feelings and bruised ego, we know something isn't right for us, but it's the idea that we're being rejected that makes us feel bad – not the actual outcome.

The universe works in mysterious ways and rejection can actually keep you from accepting jobs that would have made you miserable, settling down with partners who wouldn't have been there for you and spending time on activities or with people that don't truly align with who you are.

The next time you feel even a twinge of rejection, remind yourself that you're being redirected to something *even better*. It may feel unnatural at first, but when you start seeing rejection as the blessing it truly is, you'll stop letting it get you down. You'll be excited knowing a window of possibilities has opened and something great lies ahead. It may even show up today.

> The next time you feel even a twinge of rejection, remind yourself you are being redirected toward something **even better.**

"Love isn't finding someone to live with. It's finding someone you can't live without."

- Unknown

24.
Don't Settle for Love

Sometimes we want love so badly that the fear of not having it gets us into a lot of trouble, and we may settle for the wrong person. It's not like finding that special someone with what the French call *je ne sais quoi* (a quality that can't be described) always happens on our timelines.

Even the most optimistic people can fall prey to the lows of holding out for their person. What single person hasn't at one point found themselves home alone on a Saturday night sipping a glass of wine and reaching out to an ex, just to, you know, see if perhaps you could've been mistaken and they weren't in fact a narcissistic ass? Or, wondered if you should just give that persistent person you met a chance because, after all, they *are* nice and probably would make a great partner – even though you're not attracted to them in the slightest?

When it comes to love, it's never a good idea to move forward with reservations – whether you're not totally feeling it, you know you deserve to be treated better or your gut questions if there's a better fit somewhere out there.

"Well," we tell ourselves, "No one's perfect and I *really* want to settle down."

No one *is* perfect, but there's a feeling in your stomach that something's off.

"He's not the one for me," an inner voice whispers, but you *shh* it away because, well, he's right here in front of you and you want it all to work out so badly.

No person or relationship is flawless, but if someone doesn't feel completely right for you in your bones, if someone isn't treating you as wonderfully as you know you deserve, or if someone can't give you what you truly want, love yourself enough to walk away.

There's no need to settle in order to settle down.

25.
Enjoy Your Solo Time

When single, it's easy to get wrapped up in fears that you'll be alone forever or feel anxious that you're falling behind in life and you miss out on all there is to love about this time. But what if you knew in six months, you'd meet that special someone and be together for the rest of your life? Would you spend your single days as you are?

One weekend of every month my friend Jenna's husband travels for work. She tells him she hates to see him go, but secretly she's thrilled that for the next 48 hours she can indulge in her former single ways.

Jenna kicks off the weekend with a night at home watching whatever TV she wants (no compromises necessary!), while ordering whatever takeout she's in the mood for. The next night, she hits the town with friends, relishing the freedom of knowing she doesn't have to tip-toe into bed or worry about being too loud when turning the kitchen upside-down making a mean, midnight grilled cheese sandwich. Jenna loves her husband, but the truth is, no matter how great the relationship, there are certain single perks even the happiest of marrieds hate to part with.

The world is your playground when you're single. You can travel to any place that calls you and make your desires top priority. You never know when you'll have a run-in with love, (quite literally sometimes!) and your relationship status changes forever. So, whether you are single by intention or not, do yourself a favor and enjoy this time to the fullest. Your future self will thank you for it later.

26.
Be on the Same Page With People You Date

When dating someone new, we can get so wrapped up in how the person feels about us, that we forget to consider how we feel about them. We get swept away by excitement and butterflies and often wonder (and even worry) if they like us when we should be asking ourselves, "Is this person really a good match *for me*?"

Dating, relationships and all things love can be downright messy at times. But knowing what you want, and partnering with someone who wants the same, will spare both people drama, confusion and even resentment. It will also keep you from abandoning those things you want for your life that are *truly* important to you.

Be honest …

Do you want a serious partnership or a casual one? Is having kids, pets and a family important to you? Do you want to settle down in a small town or a big city, or spend your time traveling the globe?

Be real with yourself about what you want and date people who are on the same page.

If being in a committed partnership is important to you, resist getting romantically involved with anyone who doesn't want that too. It sounds simple, but I don't know one person who hasn't at some point tried to make something work with someone who *did not* want that same thing!

"Do you want to be in a relationship or do you want to be with this person?" friends ask when we find ourselves in limbo with someone.

"I want to be in a relationship with this person!" We answer knowing deep down that's not an option, but we've come to believe they're the only person in the entire world we're capable of having a relationship with – it doesn't matter that they don't feel the same.

If you and the person you're getting involved with want different things, cut the cord and move on. It's easier said than done, but doing so will save you both unnecessary drama, confusion and heartache. So, if you're dating for fun, let them know before their heart gets invested. And if you're serious about having a true partnership with rings and "I do's," don't get romantically involved with anyone who doesn't want that too.

Keep in mind, if someone wants to jump off your boat, the best thing you can do is say, "Bon Voyage" and keep sailing in the direction of your destination. Don't change course or steer circles around them. Don't try to entice them back with messages or manipulation. If they want to come back, they'll make it known and at that point you can decide how you feel, and if they don't, well, you have an open seat for an even better first mate to come aboard.

Trying to have a relationship with someone who is incapable of giving you one is like pulling into a gas station to buy fresh sushi. There's a slim chance you may find it, but it sure as hell isn't the easy way!

You deserve to have everything you wish for in love, and there really are tons of fish in the sea.

> *"Love is a game that two can play and both can win."*
> - Eva Gabor

27.
Love the One You're With

Being happy with someone who is your best friend and lover all rolled into one is one of the best feelings in life. But no matter how magical a relationship is in the beginning, there comes a point when the butterflies wane, the excitement fades and actual work comes into play.

Relationships are like gardens; they require maintenance in order to flourish. While every relationship is different, here are a few universal keys to help you stick together:

Remember, you're on the same team

You and your partner make up a team, so there's no need to create competition between one another or kick the other down. Instead of bad-mouthing your teammate, do what you can to build each other up and be one another's biggest supporters. Be kind and loving, and ask for the same in return.

Remember that when you're good to your partner, it not only helps them, it helps you too because you two are a team.

Be appreciative

Remember how grateful you were in the beginning not just to have a partner, but to have *them* as a partner? Give thanks out loud to one another each day for how they make your life better. Whether it's pouring you a cup of coffee in the morning, giving you a warm hug, making a grocery run or putting the kids to bed at night, take note of all of it. When you give your attention to what's going well, you tend to see more of it. And if you are complimenting your other half for all they do, they'll probably want to do more of those nice things.

We all want to feel valued, especially by our partners. Showing appreciation is one of the easiest ways to keep a relationship healthy and sadly the one we tend to forget about most.

Be affectionate

Babies need touch in order to survive during their early weeks of life. Relationships need touch in order to survive a lifetime. Whether it's holding hands while watching TV, exchanging quick kisses when passing in the hallway or taking a moment to hold one another under the stars before doing the dishes, remember to be affectionate with your partner.

Years may roll by, but the importance of sex in a relationship doesn't. It's common for relationships to be filled with steamy, gotta-have-you-right-now moments in the beginning, but fast-forward a few years or decades and the sexual landscape changes quite a bit. It actually takes planning and effort. Work's exhausting, there's laundry to be folded and screaming kids aren't exactly aphrodisiacs!

Having a good sex life is one of the best ways to connect and reconnect with your partner, so do what you can to keep a little fire burning in your relationship. It may not always be easy, but it's worth the effort.

Fight fair

Every healthy couple fights. It's not *if* you fight but *how* you fight that will either strengthen or destroy a relationship. Make an effort to fight fair and be accountable for the part you play too. When talking things out, come from an *I* point of view, "I feel … I don't care for … I don't feel good about …" instead of attacking your partner with "you, you, you!"

A relationship is a delicate dance and timing is everything. Be considerate of what's going on in your partner's life when you *do* drop an argument bomb and be sure to show up with an open mind.

Return to the beginning

Falling in love is the best feeling. It's like a smile is plastered to your face and nothing else matters. It's natural that these feelings fade, but one of the best ways to reignite a relationship is to close our eyes and remember how it played out in the first act.

Sip a glass of wine under the stars with your partner and return to the beginning. Share with each other how you felt when you first connected. Reminisce about how you met and fell in love, and everything about them that you loved from the start. Think of it like giving your car battery a jumpstart – the more you feel those good feelings, the more you'll continue feeling the love.

It's easy to forget how good we have it sometimes, but the grass isn't always greener on the other side. Chances are, there's a lot of love between you and your partner, even on the days that feel tough. Do your best to treat each other how you want to be treated, stay on the same team and keep that spark alive. Love is a gift and good things are worth working on.

28.
Have Your Own Life Outside of a Relationship

There's a scene in the movie *Runaway Bride* that always comes to mind when I think about having our own lives outside of a relationship. Richard Gere's character is confronting Julia Roberts' character and questioning her love for her soon-to-be husband.

"You're so lost you don't even know what kind of eggs you like!" he shouts, pointing out how with each of her ex's she claimed to like her morning eggs how they did – scrambled, fried, poached, or egg whites only.

"That's called changing your mind," Julia Roberts' character replies.

Then comes the part that always sticks with me.

"No, that's called not having a mind of your own!"

Relationships are about two separate individuals sharing one life in harmony. We're bound to compromise and blend together. But sometimes we compromise so much for so long that we end up compromising ourselves. It's not uncommon for a couple to do an activity together, say golf, and years (and a closet full of golf attire) later one person wakes up and says, "Come to think of it, I don't actually like golf!"

We often do things our partners enjoy that we don't particularly care for because we want to spend time with the person we love. But over time, all of the seemingly insignificant, "I don't care, whatever you want," and "Sure, that sounds good," lines can add up to a significant loss of ourselves.

Building a life with a partner is a beautiful blessing, but no matter how amazing the relationship and how much you adore them, you must always have your *own* life.

Whether it's regular lunches with friends, a career you're passionate about or taking watercolor painting classes, having activities, dreams and goals that are separate from our partner help us retain a sense of identity. It keeps us committed to our own happiness and also gives us the opportunity to miss those we consider our better halves.

Having your own life provides talking points too, because let's face it, in the beginning, most relationships are filled with evenings on roof decks that turn into watching the sunrise as there's just so much to discover about one another. Fast-forward a few years, and those lengthy conversations are often replaced with the mundane, "How was your day?" "Good and yours?" ruts that fall upon every couple from time to time.

It's easy to lose sight of our goals when we're excited about love, but healthy relationships are those that give you permission to expand your life and seize your dreams. They aren't meant to shrink you. No matter how wonderful your relationship, take time to reconnect with who you are and figure out what you want to accomplish next in your own life.

Ask yourself, "Who am *I*?" and "How do I like *my* eggs?"

*"Sometimes good things fall apart
so even better things can fall together."*
- Marilyn Monroe

29.
Go Easy After a Breakup

Breakups are hard and messy and take a toll on everyone involved. They can bring out the worst in us and even take on a life of their own. In the blink of an eye, a spark turns into a blazing fire and just like that a relationship becomes too far gone to ever get back. After the embers settle, we wake up as if it had all been a really bad dream and say to ourselves, *"What the hell just happened?!"*

It's amazing how we can be so close to someone and share every moment, laugh and inside joke, and then something changes and we become less to each other than strangers passing on the street. Much like with a physical death, breakups are accompanied by stages of grief and bring along a variety of emotions.

When you're navigating a breakup or dealing with an emotional hangover, give yourself permission to cry, be blue, scream or do whatever you need to allow yourself to feel all you do. Let it all come up and out of your system. Just keep in mind this process is supposed to help you move on with your life, not become a *new way* of life, so give yourself a timeline to stay in bed or talk about nothing else if you need to.

Breakups can be hard on our bodies and while that bottle of wine and gallon of ice cream may look tempting, do your best to be extra good to yourself right now. Think bubble baths, massages, walks to clear your head and long talks with good friends who love and support you.

Prioritize rest and wellness, be patient and go easy. Make it a point to enjoy the simple things that make you smile, like a good novel or comforting TV series. Most importantly, take this time to invest all that love you gave to your partner back into yourself. The relationship broke, but it doesn't have to break you.

It can be downright painful when a relationship doesn't work out how you want it to, but no matter how blindsided or destroyed you may feel, we all eventually emerge from the dark side of the tunnel. Instead of taking it personally or trying to "fix" something, take off your rose-colored glasses and make a list of everything you want in a partner. Each person we're with gives us the chance to refine our request to Cupid for the kind of relationship we want for the long haul. Even the duds and disappointments (it happens!) provide contrast, so you can know with even more certainty what you want next. It could even be your ex, but an improved version and an upgraded relationship.

Some partners come into our lives for a reason or a season, and that's all they're meant to stay for. Sometimes we need to recognize that when the season changes, it's OK to let them go. It's OK to say goodbye. Even to people who have at one point meant everything to us.

> *"We travel, initially, to lose ourselves; and we travel, next to find ourselves."*
>
> \- Pico Iyer

30.
Travel Solo

I was speaking on a panel and a woman in the audience asked me what I'd recommend everyone try at least once in their lifetime. My answer surprised even myself:

"Travel solo."

I never planned on falling in love with traveling solo. I never imagined it would change my life in ways I didn't even know possible when I embarked on my first journey.

Six months after a heartbreak left me devastated, I found myself in that serene place where my tears had ceased, my heart had mended and I knew I was going to be OK. With all of this in mind though, I still wasn't quite ready for a relationship. I thought I was and gave it a shot only to find out that I had love baggage in tons!

When I tried to have love again with a really great guy who was nothing but good to me, it was clear I wasn't ready. I was still fragile. I was untrusting and my insecurities ran high. I had morphed into a version of myself I never intended, nor did I like – a distrusting, paranoid person always waiting for the other shoe to drop. In my case, to be cheated on again. Long gone was the light-hearted, optimistic, secure woman I had once been.

I had lost myself and I knew that in order to be in a healthy, happy relationship in the future, I had some figuring out to do. The only person I needed to date was myself.

I took time off of my junior year of college, borrowed airline miles from my parents and enrolled myself in a language school in Florence, Italy. Since my last name is Florence, I figured what better place to find myself than in a city with my own name!

The first couple of months I lived in a flat with seven other language students. I was the only American. The next few months I traveled everywhere I could.

At 20 years old, I hadn't done much alone up until that point. Certainly nothing like traveling halfway across the world through countries where I barely knew the language. Everything about the experience: traveling solo, meeting new people, seeing other ways of living, learning how to depend on myself, going out to dinner by myself, not complaining because I didn't have anyone to complain to – it changed me to my core.

Here I was making friends with people from all over the world, crossing countries on trains and hauling luggage around Europe *all by myself*. It challenged me and I loved every minute of it. With responsibility for myself came freedom. I could spend hours at the Colosseum in Rome, the Louvre in Paris or journaling at a quaint café in the heart of Tuscany. Depending on myself gave me a sense of accomplishment. I could take care of myself. I could experience joy in every day *all by myself.*

Even the moments that tested me gave me no choice but to dig deep and find the strength to keep going, and to know when I needed help and not be afraid to ask for it.

Like anyone who's traveled solo knows, lonely times were inevitable. Sometimes they rolled in like a set of waves that were steady and slow to pass. Other times, they knocked me off my feet, leaving me gasping for breath. But I learned fast that even though we may speak different languages and have various ways of going about life, every person on this planet has more in common than not. We're all humans seeking joy and love and are here for one another. And the days I spent exploring by myself or eating dinner at a table for one made me realize how I could be alone and not feel lonely.

Somewhere between the canals of Venice and the cobblestone streets of Paris, I discovered my own resilience. I had met me, a new me. I liked me. No matter what life would throw my way, I knew I would be OK. And once I came into that place, as if on cue, I met someone new – and magic swirled around us.

Whether you want to reconnect with yourself or connect truly for the first time in your life, or if you need space to clear your head, unpack emotions, or simply to have an adventure, traveling solo will teach you more about yourself than you ever imagined. It will challenge and enchant you and make you a stronger, wiser and more confident version of yourself.

What's more, you'll have a collection of great stories to share at those dinners when you're *not* all by yourself!

"Time you enjoy wasting is not wasted time."
- Marthe Troly-Curtin

31.
Savor the Sweetness of Doing Nothing

There's a saying in Italy, "Dolce far niente." Translated it means, *the sweetness of doing nothing*. I was introduced to this saying by an Italian gentleman who I had the pleasure of sharing a bench with one crisp October afternoon in Cinque Terre, Italy.

It's becoming rare these days to do nothing. Even when we don't have anywhere to be or anything pressing to see, it's unlikely we simply sit and watch people pass by on the street or stare off into the clouds. More often, we reach for our phones and fall into the digital world.

Italians understand the value in doing nothing. They know when our heads aren't looking down at our phones the world right in front of us opens up (as well as conversations with delightful Italian gentlemen!). They also know that turning off and tuning out is restorative for our bodies and minds, and keeps us living in the present.

In Italy, it's not uncommon for restaurants and shops to hang a sign saying "Closed for Vacation." for an entire month. They know life is better when we're not fully consumed by work and busyness, and they make time for vacations and pleasure. Whether it's exploring a new place in the world, taking an afternoon stroll hand-in-hand with a partner or sipping a cappuccino in a café after lunch, Italians know our life purpose is to enjoy as much as possible.

No matter where you live in this wonderful world, take a cue from our Italian friends and make time to enjoy the sweetness of doing nothing. Just be sure to leave your phone (and any guilt!) behind.

32.
Make Someone Smile

There's nothing better than making someone feel good, and there are so many ways we can brighten up a person's day.

Make it a point to bring a smile to someone's face each day and:

Give a compliment.

Give a hug.

Give a shout-out to a friend for the amazing person they are and for all they do.

Give something you never use to someone who will get use out of it.

Give up a grudge.

Give an extra "I love you" to your partner, kids, fur babies and friends who make your life the beautiful, (though sometimes wild!) ride it is.

Give a dollar or what you can to a local charity or someone in your community who needs it.

Give a big "Thank You!" to someone who has helped you out and been a saving grace.

Give your time to help a friend or neighbor who can use a hand.

Give yourself a break and a hug for who you are and for all you do. You may not be perfect, but you're doing your best and deserve to give yourself some love and appreciation.

We get what we give in life and when you smile the world smiles back. :-)

*"The intuitive mind is
where our genius resides."*
- Angela Artemis

33.
Trust Your Intuition

Our intuition is like a secret weapon. When we listen to it and follow it, this guiding light can spare us pain, sorrow and sometimes regret. It can even save our lives by telling us to make an appointment with the doctor or to get a second opinion.

We're all blessed with intuition. Whether you've mastered it or your signal is coming in a little too fuzzy, here are three ways to strengthen your intuition and tune in:

Talk to yourself

Take a long drive or a walk around the neighborhood and talk to yourself out loud about what's on your mind. Risk looking like a weirdo and have a full-blown conversation with yourself. This may sound silly, but when you talk to yourself out loud you hear your thoughts in a way that's easier to digest and you get a better idea of what's really going on. You can gain an amazing amount of clarity and relief when you get it all out.

Have quiet time each day

Our minds are filled with chatter that can get in the way of our inner voice, especially when it's only speaking at a whisper. Give yourself 10-20 minutes each day to be quiet and alone with your thoughts. Drive to pick up the kids from school in silence, meditate, take pen to paper and journal, or sip a cup of coffee and stare into the sky. Answers often lie deep within us so be still and listen to the wise voice inside you – it's in there and knows what it's talking about.

Check-in with your body

Our bodies are like incredible search engines that we can tune into for answers. When you're at a crossroad and a decision needs to be made, your body will help show you the way.

Do you feel peaceful or excited when you think about something? Do you feel hesitant, unsure or have a heavy feeling in your stomach? Feeling light usually means something is right, so pay attention to how your body feels and let it guide you.

Following your intuition can feel inconvenient at times. After all, switching jobs or moving to a new town can be scary and takes effort, even when something inside of you is saying, "It's time for a change." And our minds can be really clever at talking us out of something even when we know in our bones it's the right call.

Your gut instinct knows what's best for you, even if it eclipses logic or lengthy pro and con lists. It may seem like the harder option, but trust your intuition and follow your inner guide.

34.
Be OK With People Not Liking You

You weren't put on this planet to please everyone. You are here to please *you*. While it's human nature to want everyone to like us, with billions of beings on the planet, we're bound to encounter people who don't care for us all that much for whatever reason, or for no reason at all.

The problem with caring so much about being liked is when we go out of our way to try and win appreciation from someone. It can put your self-confidence in their hands – and no one should have that much power over you.

It can also be dangerous when we hold ourselves back from being who we truly are, or from doing something that matters to us, because we're afraid of rejection or criticism.

Whether it's someone you want to date, a co-worker, your best friend's other best friend, an in-law or someone on social media, instead of putting effort into getting someone to like you, ask yourself, "Do I really like this person?" Because there's a good chance you may not actually be a fan. And there's no need to spend your time and energy trying to "win over" someone who, when you think about it, you don't really care for anyway.

You'll never be able to control what other people think about you, so make peace with the fact that not everyone will think you're awesome and let their opinions roll on by. **Instead of caring so much about what other people think of you, start caring more about what *you* think of you.** Keep focusing on your side of the street and on being the best version of yourself you can be.

Release the need to be liked by everyone and you will be free.

35.
Be OK With Not Liking Everyone

Chances are you're a good person, and you may think being a good person means you need to be friends with everyone. But it's perfectly OK *not* to be.

There's no need to hate on or badmouth people (it's an unproductive use of your time and energy!), but you're not required to spend your time with anyone who you simply don't vibe with. Like those people who make you question yourself or you feel nervous around. People who have toxic energy that leaves you feeling exhausted. People who pressure you or who you feel like you can't be your true and total self with.

When someone wants to be in your life it can feel like you have to invite them in – especially if you were raised to be a "good boy" or a "good girl." But not everyone you cross paths with may be as kind-hearted as you are. Chances are at some point you'll encounter people who don't have your best interest at heart. People who may throw you under the bus, take advantage of you and be "takers" rather than "givers."

If you don't feel like someone is truly good for you or you don't feel happy when you're around them, know that you don't need to put yourself in any situation that will make you feel uncomfortable. You have life's full permission to be choosy and to opt out of invites or excuse yourself early.

If something feels off with someone, trust your gut over any voice in your head telling you to "be nice." Don't answer the phone. Don't accept the offer, invite or date. Don't get in the car. Don't open the door.

Your time and energy are precious, and you know those people who make you feel your best when you're around them. Reserve yourself for people who lift you up and don't worry about the rest.

> *"Sometimes our stop-doing list needs to be bigger than our to-do list."*
> - Patti Digh

36.
Make Space in Your Calendar

We feel more relaxed when our calendar has open space. Knowing we have plenty of time and flexibility to do what needs to get done allows us to breathe deeper and enjoy ourselves far more.

We often accept a hectic schedule as "it is what it is," but life doesn't have to be this way, at least not every day.

Be honest …

Do you *have* to bake cupcakes for your book club when you can pick up a dozen ready-made ones at the store?

Does that package *have* to be mailed today or can it wait until tomorrow?

Do you *have* to go to your neighbor's BBQ that you're not even looking forward to?

Even when we think everything on our to-do list is a must, there's almost always something you don't really *have* to do. Or, something you can say "no" to, move to another day, outsource or cross off altogether.

> It can be easy to fall into the trap of thinking that a busy schedule makes you a successful person, but the *true* great accomplishment in life is having time in your day to enjoy yourself.

One of the best ways to feel happier and experience more ease is to make choices that will uncomplicate your life. Be intentional about creating more open space in your calendar by prioritizing what's an absolute must and taking shortcuts, getting help with or saying "no" to what's not. Spend more time and energy on those things that truly matter and less on things that don't. Once you give up a few daily to-dos and get comfortable saying "no" to draining requests, pay attention to how you feel. Chances are, you'll appreciate that you can catch your breath and turn some attention to your own well-being.

It can be easy to fall into the trap of thinking that a busy schedule makes you a successful person, but the *true* great accomplishment in life is having time in your day to enjoy yourself. Be aware of how much you take on and do what you can to create more open space in your calendar to just be.

37.
Honor Your Life Seasons

We'd never expect this incredible planet we call home to cram fall, winter, spring and summer into one, but often, we humans expect ourselves to take on so many big projects, all at the same time. We stack hat after hat on our heads thinking we can do it all. And the truth is, we *can* do it all – just not all at once.

Life is about seasons and taking on too much at once is a recipe for stress. When we honor the season we're in by giving our full attention to only a few things, we make more progress and feel more enjoyment and satisfaction.

When I set out to write this book, I had four ongoing work projects consuming a great deal of my time and energy and a full social calendar. At the same time, my good friend Mia was starting a fitness routine with a huge goal, taking care of a newborn and adjusting to motherhood, working part time and planning a home renovation project. We both also had daily life responsibilities including taking care of homes, family, pets, finances, cooking, cleaning, etc.

My friends and I often lead parallel lives, and when Mia and I met up for lunch one day we both knew that trying to tackle so many things at the same time wasn't working. We were spread thin, overwhelmed and instead of making real progress in any one area, neither of us were making headway on anything and feeling real bad about it.

To get and remain in the zone – whether it's writing a book or raising a new human, often sacrifices have to be made. You can't do everything at once, so you have to pick and choose what's most important and learn to say "no" or "not now" to other things vying for your attention.

I'll be honest, even though I wanted to give my full attention to this book, it wasn't easy to press pause on other things. The first few weeks in fact, I felt like I "should" be doing everything. But stepping away from other projects and areas of my social life was the only way I was going to finish writing it this century (even when my days started before sunrise!). And instead of my mind being scattered in different directions, I yearned for mental space to focus only on this book. Because when we focus on less, we actually accomplish more. I also wanted to be fully present to enjoy the process more.

If you're multi-passionate (or impatient), it can be challenging to focus on only one or two things. It's not always an option either. Sometimes you *do* have to raise a toddler, work a full-time job, care for an elderly family member and deal with moving all at the same time.

But day-to-day life is a lot, so when you add something new to the mix, even if it's something you're excited about, be realistic about how much you can take on and avoid biting off more than you can chew in any life season. Maybe this is the season you focus on your health and lifestyle improvements, or the season you focus on raising a kind human being. Perhaps this is the time to commit fully to a new job, start a business, learn a new language, or put yourself out there to make new friends.

Instead of trying to cram everything you want to tackle into one season, spread things out across a month, quarter, year or longer. Focus on what's most important in this current life season and set the rest aside for now.

Nature doesn't hurry or rush and everything gets accomplished in its own perfect way. Be present with the life season you are in from start to completion and enjoy it as much as possible. Everything else can wait until next season.

*"Have patience with all things,
but first of all with yourself."*
- St. Francis De Sales

38.
Practice Patience

As kids, we were often told we needed to have patience. Patience when learning how to ride a bike, or how to tie our shoes. Patience in finishing up a school year and in becoming another year older so we can do all the things grown-ups do.

But life is different than it was even two decades ago. The pace has sped up rapidly and there are many things we don't have to wait for. We no longer have to patiently watch ads that interrupt our TV shows or wait weeks by the mailbox for something to arrive. Instant downloads and same-day delivery has become the new normal.

While all of this instant-ness makes life easier, it's gotten us out of the habit of practicing patience. So much so, that many of us have become increasingly less patient with ourselves. We want to be millionaires a year after starting a business, master a new language in a month, get over a cold in a day and tackle everything on our to-do list by noon. When we fall short, we get frustrated, question our capabilities or abandon goals before even giving them a fair shot.

It's important to be patient with our bodies, minds and the spirit of who we are too. If you've gone through a stressful situation or a trauma, you may need time to balance and heal your nervous system. Be gentle and nourish yourself with lots of rest, extra nutritious food and relaxation. While you may want to be able to snap your fingers and be "over" something and back to your usual self, your body, mind and nervous system may require time to recover.

In a world of instant gratification, remember to have patience with yourself and others. Be realistic about timelines for reaching goals or learning something new and don't be so quick to quit when something takes longer than you hoped for. Instead of racing toward the finish line, try to appreciate the process of growing, learning and changing.

Good things take time and there really is joy in the journey.

39.
Take a Daily Moment of Joy

How often do you do something in your day for the pure sake of enjoying yourself?

Happiness happens when we prioritize it. Instead of choosing pleasure *only after* everything else gets done, start making room in your calendar for a daily moment of joy. Even 15 minutes will do.

Perhaps you:

Take a walk in nature.

Nibble a piece of chocolate with no distractions.

Pour a glass of wine or iced tea and read a chapter in a good book.

Take a float in the ocean, lake or a pool.

Have a good laugh with an old friend.

Tend to your garden.

Play fetch with your pup.

Watch an episode of a feel-good TV show.

Your moment of joy can be anything. It's all about doing something each day that brings a smile to your face.

"Always be a first-rate version of yourself and not a second-rate version of somebody else."
- Judy Garland

40.
Be True to Yourself

Growing up, June Allyson, an award-winning actress and Hollywood legend, lived up the road from me. Famous for her sunny personality, June captured America's hearts with her sweet smile and iconic roles, playing Jo in the original film *Little Women* and Constance in *The Three Musketeers*. To me, she was simply my nice neighbor who had paper dolls made after her.

June's husband David had a role in my brother Brent's first film that he wrote, directed and acted in fresh out of graduating from USC film school. One day, while visiting the set, June was so excited about the film that she asked my brother to write her into the script to be part of the project and fun, too.

It was a hot summer day, and June and I sat in the shade between scenes gabbing about life and love. June recalled stories of Hollywood's golden age and shared what it was *really* like to be a leading lady during a time when studios and much of Hollywood was run by men.

She told me how from the moment she arrived in Hollywood, and even after she "made it," producers, studio executives and industry folks would frequently tell her who to date, how to speak, what to look like and how to be. She was constantly being told to change, whether it was her hair, teeth, voice fluctuations – the list went on. That's when she shared with me a piece of advice that I knew I'd never forget:

"Don't ever change anything about yourself for someone else, Emily." June said. "If you want to change something for you, by all means go ahead. But don't change who you are to please someone else, or to be someone they want you to be."

June gave me a wink with her cheerful smile and we walked over to the tent to get a bite to eat with the cast and crew, before returning to film what would end up being her final scene for the big screen.

We often need a reminder of just how important it is to stay honest to who we truly are. Because even though we don't mean to, sometimes we change parts of ourselves, or bottle up thoughts and points-of-view that make us, well, us.

We take passes at following our dreams, we hang out with people who don't fully accept us as we are, and we do things that don't always feel right to us. We play small, go quiet instead of standing up for ourselves and what we believe in, and even nod our head in agreement when deep inside, we don't agree at all.

In this day and age, there's no shortage of judgment and shaming. Mix that with our human desire to be liked, and it's easy to lose sight of who we *really* are and what we *truly* believe. Instead, we play life safe by trying to blend in or following someone else's lead.

Throughout life, people may try to change you or mold you to be someone other than who you intrinsically are. But like June Allyson told me that hot summer day on set, don't change anything about yourself for someone else. Have the courage and confidence to be who you are.

The purpose of life isn't to be more like everyone else. It's to be more like your authentic self.

41.
Know How Much You Matter

There are so many big players in this world that it can be easy to feel small or unimportant. You may feel like what you do isn't significant, or what you say doesn't make an impact. That's why you have to go out of your way to build yourself up and keep your belief in yourself fully charged. Because you matter today – you matter every day.

You matter to your friends.

You matter to your family.

You matter to your kids and fur babies.

You matter to the stranger you smile and say, "Good Morning" to on your daily walk.

You matter to this world.

If you feel like you're not showing up as great as you are meant to, or if you're ready to be a braver, more potent version of yourself, the time is ripe to step up and play bigger.

Whether it's through work, community causes or simply allowing yourself to be who you truly are, you are meant to let your greatness shine.

You're here for a reason, and you have a lot to offer this world, so believe in the person you are and the person you are becoming.

You make this world a better place, and you matter more than you may know.

42.
Remember, You Know What's Best for You

At times we let outsiders influence our lives more than they should. We put people on pedestals: Celebrities, Politicians, Spiritual and Religious Leaders, Teachers, Social Media Influencers – often people we've never met in real life, and truthfully, know very little about. We believe what they say even if at our core it doesn't feel right for us.

There's no one-size-fits-all roadmap for life. Just because something is right for one person doesn't mean it's right for you too. It can be helpful to receive advice and guidance, but if we give too much weight to other people's opinions, we risk silencing our own inner voice. Without meaning to, all of the "you should do this" and "you should do that" can make it nearly impossible to trust what your heart is telling you.

Don't make anyone greater than you, no matter how great they may seem to be. And be sure to always do what feels right for you – and not because someone told you to (including what you're reading, right here).

You know yourself better than anyone else does, and you really do know what's best for you.

> *"Too many people spend money they haven't earned, to buy things they don't want, to impress people that they don't like."*
> — Will Rogers

43.
Have a Healthy Relationship With Money

Like it or not, money plays a big role in our lives. We make dozens of decisions around it daily, from the food we buy, to where we live, what we wear, and even how we get from here to there. Money impacts our lives and we need to have a healthy relationship with it.

Like a friend, if we want money to be good to us, we have to be good to it, too. We need to treat it with respect and be thankful for it. This means not talking bad about money, or blaming it for aspects of our lives we don't like, or taking it for granted. It means understanding how much money we need each month to live how we want to. It also means looking forward to its arrival, celebrating when it's extra good to us, being forgiving when it doesn't show up how or when we want it to, and not holding on so tightly that we cringe every time we pay a bill.

It's important not to fall into the trap of thinking that money is bad or evil. Because it's not. It's the people who abuse it who are. And while it's true that some wealthy people do greedy, bad things in order to have more money, some people without money do those things too.

Many people desire more money and there are several ways to increase your savings. You can earn more, spend less, and invest wisely to name a few. But in order to feel more financially empowered, or to have the money you need to buy a home, travel the world, pay off debts or donate to good causes, you need to have a healthy relationship with it.

Money won't buy you happiness, kiss you goodnight or make you laugh when you're feeling low, but like it or not, it's a part of life, and the better you treat money, the more it will show up and take care of you.

44.
Clear Out Your Clutter

Clutter can make us feel chaotic, overwhelmed and even out of control. Too much stuff, and stuff we hold onto that no longer makes us happy (or perhaps never did!), not only takes up physical space, but weighs on us emotionally, too.

Eliminate clutter in your home, office and car by going through your closets and shelves yearly. Like Marie Kondo advises in her bestselling book, *The Life-Changing Magic of Tidying Up*, ask yourself if an item "sparks joy" – and if the answer is "no" then let it go.

Be honest with yourself: Have you ever used that coffee mug shaped like a fish? Do you still wear those four-inch heels you bought five years ago? Do you truly need 20 pairs of socks?

Toss out knick-knacks. Rev up the paper shredder and bid adieu to anything that no longer fits your life or makes you smile. You can even make some money selling stuff that doesn't bring you joy, but might for someone else.

Once you feel the freedom of decluttering, vow to keep your space simplified by adopting the 30-day rule before making any new non-essential purchases. Instead of buying on the fly, write down what you want on a piece of paper and place it on your desk. If after 30 days you still want the item, and you have a need for it, go for it. But chances are, you'll forget about it long before.

Increase peace and calm in your life by simplifying your surroundings. Your mind and wallet will thank you for it.

"There is no Wi-Fi in the forest, but I promise you will find a better connection."
- Ralph Smart

45.
Spend Time in Nature

Nature provides us a much-needed escape from our chaotic world. We gain perspective and are reminded there's something out there far greater than ourselves.

Spending time in nature makes us feel good. Maybe it's the dirt beneath our shoes when we're hiking in the mountains or the sand between our toes when we're walking on the beach that grounds us. Perhaps it's the sound of birds, rustling leaves or crashing waves that invigorates us.

Nature is a gift that constantly delights us. We see a rainbow in the sky and instantly smile. We witness a whale breaching from the ocean and jump with excitement. There's a whole world of incredible animals living in the mountains, beneath the sea, and in lakes and streams that take us back to basics and enchant us. The butterfly that flutters over our heads, the deer that moves with a surreal combination of both power and grace, the baby chicks that chirp in chorus. How they live in the present, relying on instinct and detached from technology and superficialities, inspires us.

Make it a point to step away from it all and into the peace of nature. Watch the sky turn colors at sunset and enjoy the clouds rolling by. Let your mind wander as you soak up the sights, sounds and smells. Just be sure to be good to nature in return. Respect her, and do your best to protect her as a "thank you" for all the beauty and wonder she gives us.

46.
Be Good to Mother Earth

When we all stayed home during the pandemic, pollution in city skies lifted, the canals of Venice became clear and ocean reefs flourished. We humans impact our planet Earth and we need to do our part to care for and mother our home.

Chances are you're already doing what you can to give Mother Earth more TLC, but here are some things we can do that together will make a positive impact:

- Bring your own reusable grocery bags to the store.
- Use only reef-safe sunscreen when you go in the ocean.
- Batch errands and plan ahead. Save money on gas and air pollution by doing grocery store runs once a week instead of daily.
- Use cloth napkins instead of paper towels.
- If you buy soda or anything that comes in a 6-pack with plastic around the tops, take scissors to the plastic loops

and cut them up so sea turtles, birds and other wildlife don't get caught in them.

- Conserve water by turning off the faucet when you brush your teeth.
- When you're on the go use a refillable water bottle and ditch plastic bottles.
- Volunteer or donate to organizations that protect our wildlife and friends under the sea.
- Plant trees or donate to organizations that help remove carbon dioxide from the air.
- Be choosy with your money and only buy from companies that care about the planet and animals as much as you do.
- Consider how much you personally contribute to waste and make an effort to contribute less. Before buying something new, think about how much you truly need it, whether you can buy it used, and also where it will end up in five or even 10 years.

We only have one planet, and not only does she provide us so much joy, but we depend on her for our survival. So, let's be kinder to Mother Earth and do what we can to give her all that she gives us.

47.
Re-Think Success

In my 20s, I was hot on the heels of what up until that point I'd deemed success. I was working at one of the top PR agencies in Beverly Hills, immersed in the glitz and glamor of red carpets, A-list celebrities, exclusive events and media galore.

On the outside my job looked sexy with inside scoops and VIP perks, but inside, it was draining the life out of me. It sucked up so much time and energy there was but a drop left for friends and family, not to mention personal hobbies or self-care. Truth-be-told, the only satisfaction I had was when people would, "Ooh" and "Ahh" when I told them where I worked. At the end of each long day, I didn't feel all that happy or fulfilled. All I really felt was an urge to pour a great, big glass of wine!

There are pluses and minuses to all jobs, and while I love publicity and working with the media and adored the vast majority of my co-workers, many of whom are dear friends for life, after a while I couldn't shake the feeling that this wasn't a life I was meant to lead. One Sunday afternoon after another weekend lost to work, I realized all I craved was what my former landlord Joe said to me years before when we were chatting one afternoon in Boston.

"Being happy, ya know," Joe said. "That's all that matters."

You know how you nod your head and agree with someone and recognize that what they're saying is profound, but at the same time, it kind of goes in one ear and out the other? That's what happened to me that spring day talking with Joe. It was a Saturday afternoon, and I'd just returned from the market. The sun was shining, though patches of snow still lingered on the ground.

It was a day to celebrate being outdoors and a sea of tourists followed the Freedom Trail into the heart of my street in the North End, Boston's Little Italy. I navigated through the crowd, all enjoying slices of pizza and gelato on their way to Paul Revere's house and the Old North Church, and I found Joe sipping an espresso outside my doorstep. Joe's family owned a fabulous Italian Ristorante where my roommate and I lived four floors above and our front door was conveniently adjacent to their kitchen door. (Extremely convenient in winter snowstorms when we were hungry for a great meal and didn't want to brace the cold!)

After raving about the welcomed weather, I accepted Joe's offer for a glass of wine and took a seat at the single table on the sidewalk.

"Salute!" Joe and I clinked our glasses and I watched his gaze follow a black town car pulling up to the restaurant across the street. An older gentleman, still dressed for winter in a designer black trench coat and black leather gloves emerged from the sleek car carrying a briefcase.

"This guy," Joe motioned to the man now walking into the restaurant by himself. "He got nobody." Joe shook his head. "His wife left him, kids don't talk to him, lost all his friends. Only company he's got are the people who work for him. Known him 30 years and all he's ever cared about was work and money."

It was one of those stories you've heard before. A person lets work consume their whole life and now they are old and alone, just them and piles of cash.

"He has all this money," Joe continued, "but people like you and me, we have time for family, friends and for life!" He savored a sip of wine. "You tell me, who's *really* a success?"

I clinked my glass with Joe's and took a long sip of wine, but it wouldn't be until years later and 3,000 miles west when I was pulling out of the office parking garage in Beverly Hills that I finally got what he was talking about that day.

"Holy shit," I said to myself. "I am so *not* a success!"

We see it every day with friends and loved ones. We look around and people are stressed to their max. "How've you been?" We ask and they reply with something like, "Busy! Work's crazy!" Some people even seem proud of this like being busy and stressed validates their existence.

While it's amazing to experience success in a career – and we all will have times when a work project requires our full attention and extra time and energy – if you are *always* giving so much to work or chasing money or outer recognition that you don't have room to show up and be present for anyone else, or get enjoyment out of your daily life, you may want to re-think your idea of success. Especially if the work doesn't make you truly happy or fulfilled.

At my Grandma Dorothy's memorial service, I read something Ralph Waldo Emerson said about success that reminded me of how she lived her life. My Grandma Dorothy never had a big career or a fancy lifestyle. She didn't always have it easy, but she was nevertheless always eager to laugh, sing and have a ball. Emerson's definition of success is the truest I've heard:

"What is success? To laugh often and much; To win the respect of intelligent people and the affection of children; To earn the appreciation of honest critics and endure the betrayal of false friends; To appreciate the beauty; To find the best in others; To leave the world a bit better, whether by a healthy child, a garden patch or a redeemed social condition; To know even one life has breathed easier because you have lived; This is to have succeeded."

Success doesn't define us, we define success. But if you, like many people, view it as having piles of cash, power or fame, you may want to re-think what's truly important to you.

While making a living is necessary, it's important to ask yourself at what cost. Missing out on time with family and friends and people who love you? Robbing years from your life as a result of excess stress, lack of quality sleep and self-care? Not truly enjoying your one beautiful life?

Decide what success looks like for you and strive for it. Just be sure to include more time for family, friends, love and laughter in that vision. Like Joe said to me that spring day over a glass of wine in Boston, it's all that truly matters.

*"Sometimes we can only find our true direction when
we let the wind of change carry us."*
- Mimi Novic

48.
Follow the Signs

After five years of living in LA, I was ready for a change. I'd quit my publicity job to start an online company that gave me the freedom to work from anywhere, and I was craving a new town to explore, an adventure and a fresh chapter of my life. Both New York City and Marina Del Rey were calling me (and yes, Marina Del Rey is technically part of Los Angeles, but if you know the city, you'll understand it's a totally different world from where I'd been living in West Hollywood and Beverly Hills!).

New York had been a dream for a long time, but Marina Del Rey was on the ocean and would be the easier move and less scary since I already knew it well. I also hadn't forgotten how long and brutal an East Coast winter could be from when I lived in Boston.

For weeks, I made lists of pros and cons and asked family, friends, and even my local grocery store clerk, Albert, for their thoughts too. The lease was coming up on my apartment and when I had only 10 days left to decide, I fell into total panic mode.

I was sitting on my balcony, staring blankly into the distance, when my neighbor Jess called to me from next door. A few minutes later, I found myself on her balcony with a glass of wine, rambling about the pluses and minuses of each place I could move.

"I don't know, Em," Jess said after I prattled on through my entire glass of wine. "It sounds like the only thing keeping you from going to New York is fear. It may not be the easier move, but sometimes in life you have to take a leap of faith. Go to New York."

Jess had a good point, but as we said goodnight, I still wasn't ready to make a decision.

The next morning, with nine days left to decide, I walked to my local coffee house for a much-needed caffeine boost. As my self-proclaimed free-spirited barista Shelby whipped up my latte, I shared with her my dilemma.

"Why don't you give it over to God or the universe?" Shelby said and handed me my latte.

"Like how ..." I asked her, "... pray for guidance or ask for a sign?"

"Exactly!" Shelby's eyes lit up and she gave me a wink before helping the next customer in line.

I'd exhausted myself with pros and cons lists and overthinking, but I hadn't "handed it over to a higher power" or surrendered like Shelby suggested.

I walked out of the coffee house and right there on Melrose Avenue, with traffic buzzing by and horns blaring, I looked up to the sky and asked for a sign to guide me. "Please make it crystal clear where I should move to by the end of the week!" I pleaded.

What transpired over the next few days was phenomenal. The very next morning I opened the front door of my apartment to find *The New York Times* newspaper accidentally delivered to me instead of my downstairs neighbor. The next day I flipped on my car radio and Frank Sinatra's handsome voice was singing, "New York, New York" – the lyrics so seductive it felt like I was being carried out of L.A. traffic and dropped into the Big Apple. And the day after that a moving van with New York plates parked next to me at the grocery store.

All signs pointed to NYC, but, with only days left to decide, I still was on the fence. That afternoon as I drove home, I felt a strong urge to pass by my apartment and head west to Marina Del Rey. I decided to park near my friend's condo and take a stroll on the beach. I was happy to be on the sand and looking up at my friend's balcony, remembering a fun girl's night we had a few weeks before. I stayed a while squishing the sand between my toes, but something didn't feel quite right when I pictured myself living there. I looked up to the clouds above the ocean in exhausted desperation and pleaded for the higher powers to deliver a sign so big I'd know without any doubt where to move – and pronto!

Soon after, I made my way back home feeling more than ever that I wanted to be in New York. That's when I saw them. Dozens and dozens of street lamps lined Olympic Boulevard with gigantic banners hanging down with the words *Leap of Faith*. They were promoting the play coming to town, but I felt in my bones they were for me, too.

Leap of Faith. Leap of Faith.

Banner after banner I passed and my eyes teared up remembering my neighbor Jess' words from days before. "I don't know, Em. It sounds like the only thing keeping you from going to New York is fear. It may not be the easiest move, but sometimes in life you have to take a leap of faith. Go to New York."

I couldn't imagine a bigger sign reaffirming what I already knew in my heart. And with each banner I passed, my fears melted into excitement. I was moving to New York!

Weeks later, I stepped onto the plane bound for JFK airport knowing I was in for exactly what I'd been craving – a new place to explore, an adventure, a fresh chapter of my life. And the City That Never Sleeps did not disappoint.

A funny thing about fear is that it's not all the same. There's the good kind that scares yet excites you, and there's the bad kind that flat-out paralyzes you. When it comes to good fear, sometimes what we fear is exactly what we *most need* for our lives. Often, we're called to something and it's up to us to get out of our own way and step out of our comfort zone.

If you're struggling with a decision, don't feel you have to "think" your way through it or go it alone. Answers often lie deep within us, so get quiet and give yourself space to be still.

Pay attention to how you feel when you think about going in one direction over the other. Be honest with yourself about what's truly in your heart and also about what's holding you back. Even if it sounds silly, reach out to the higher powers. Ask God, the universe or your angels for clarity, neon signs or, at the very least, a nudge in the right direction.

"Whether you think you can, or you think you can't – you're right."
- Henry Ford

49.
Believe You Can

My first week in Manhattan, I covered as much of the city as possible by foot. I was subletting an apartment short-term and wanted to get a good feel for which neighborhood I'd move to more permanently. One afternoon, I wandered into the picturesque West Village and leapt, "This is where I belong!"

"Not possible," said every friend I had in the city when I told them I wanted to rent a light, bright, charming apartment in the West Village, with hardwood floors and big windows with birds chirping outside. Oh, and access to a roof deck – all at the low-budget price that I could afford.

"*Never* gonna happen." Random strangers at bars would shake their heads and give me those pity looks to remind me how green I was to NYC.

While none of this was what I wanted to hear, at least I scored a few free drinks from bartenders telling me, "Good luck with that!"

While all of these real New Yorkers knew the city far better than yours truly, I also believed Theodore Roosevelt understood what he was talking about when he said: "Believe you can and you're halfway there."

So, I gleefully brushed off their opinions, and every day I journeyed to the West Village and set up my computer at a neighborhood coffee shop to work. I imagined that I lived just around the corner in my light, bright, charming apartment, with hardwood floors, birds chirping out the large windows and of course, access to a roof deck – all at a price I could easily afford.

Days went by and turned into weeks, and then one day as the leaves began to fall, a listing appeared that matched everything I'd been dreaming of. Including the chirping birds!

Throughout life, people may tell you that something you want isn't possible. While their intentions may be good, don't let their opinions deter you. Instead, feel free to respond with, "I can and I will. Watch me!" Or, do what I do and simply let their opinions roll on by. **You can't control what someone says to you, but you do get to decide what you take away after the conversation ends.** You can let their words sink in or brush them off, understanding that just because life happened a certain way for them doesn't mean it has to play out that way for you too. No one's life experience has to become your reality.

If doubt creeps in and you start questioning yourself, or if you begin losing faith, jog your memory for those times when things worked out in your favor – even against the odds. Remember that beautiful home you found at a price you could easily afford, the wonderful partner who loved you, the time your body healed, the job you were hired for, and that day money showed up in your pocket as if by magic? If good things happened to you before, they will happen to you again.

Being pragmatic has benefits, but it's important to keep in mind that anything can happen. Even when you don't know how something will come to fruition, keep asking for what you want and expecting life to be on your side. Like the great author Dr. Wayne Dyer said, "You will see it when you believe it."

*"I like my coffee black
and my mornings bright."*
- Terri Guillemets

50.
Start Your Day in a Positive Way

In an ideal world, you'd wake up every morning and take your time easing into the day. You'd spend an hour or so exercising, meditating, journaling and eating a healthy breakfast. But chances are, your morning looks a lot different, getting the kids ready for school, taking out the dog, packing lunches and tidying the house before you dash out the door.

The morning sets the stage for what lies ahead and even if you are tight on time, it's still possible to start your day in a positive way. Here are four easy ways:

See the good

Instead of rolling out of bed thinking things like, "Ugh, I don't want to go to work today," or, "why did I have so much wine last night?!" or, "this weather blows!" find three things to be pleased with from the get-go. A good night's sleep, a cozy bed, a roof over your head, your tail-wagging dog. You get to choose what you give your attention to, so be grateful for sunny days, rainy days and for the chance to experience another day.

> You get to choose what you give your attention to, so be grateful for sunny days, rainy days and for the chance to experience another day.

Get your confidence going

Give yourself an immediate injection of self-esteem with a compliment. Find something staring back in the mirror to appreciate while you brush your teeth. Sip your coffee and remind yourself that you are a good person and doing a great job. Take a page from author Louise Hay and say to yourself, "I love and approve of myself." Be on your own winning team from the moment you wake up and tell yourself, "This is going to be a really good day!"

Gift yourself more peace

Experience more peace in your mornings by steering clear of outside noise for as long as you can. Resist diving into your phone and other tech knowing that a disturbing news story, annoying social media post, or a work email before the work day begins can spiral you out of bed and into a bad mood. Just because your phone is buzzing with alerts it doesn't mean you have to respond. Gift yourself more easygoing mornings by leaving your tech alone.

Do one thing that will make you feel good

Each morning is a fresh start so do something for yourself that you know will feel good. Even if you only have a few minutes to do it.

Choose one activity like stretching, taking a walk, meditating, reviewing your goals, sipping coffee while staring into the clouds, or journaling. You don't need to try and do *all the things*, just choose one each morning to enjoy.

Morning time is sacred time, so do what you can to start your day in a positive way. You have the rest of the day for everything else.

51.
Eliminate Life's Little Annoyances

Little things get on all of our nerves, causing us to cringe and swerve off course from an otherwise problem-free day. The window sticks, the door squeaks and the partner loudly munches chips while you're trying to work.

Little bothers reveal themselves again and again, making us huff and puff, roll our eyes and curse them under our breath. And too often we just complain, rather than eliminate these annoyances once and for all.

When something's bothering you ask yourself, "Is there anything I can do to save myself from encountering this again tomorrow?"

If the answer is "Yes," then take care of it. Call someone to fix the sticky window, go to the hardware store and buy grease for the squeaky door, and kindly ask your partner to munch chips far away from where you're working. (Or put on headphones!)

Little bothers have a way of becoming big deals and good mood killers over time, so do yourself a favor and eliminate them as soon as you can, whenever you can. Then sit back and enjoy your really good day.

52.
Tune Out Drama

There's a good chance you know someone who is always immersed in chaos or conflict. No matter the day, some kind of drama surrounds them.

When someone tells you about their dramas, be aware of how involved you become and be careful not to let their problems consume you. It's important to be there for people in life, but overextending yourself or sacrificing your own inner peace doesn't help you *or* them.

Try not to get sucked into your own inner dramas, either. Our minds are capable of creating wild stories and becoming obsessive about certain situations, often blowing them *way* out of proportion! Have you ever been showering or whipping up breakfast and, all of a sudden, you're fully engaged in an imaginary conversation with someone? Or you're playing out a dramatic scenario that's *never* going to happen in real life?

Our minds can swoop us out of the present and drop us smack into the middle of an imaginary dramatic situation where we experience all kinds of self-inflicted anger, hurt and frustration. So when you notice your mind is churning up drama, stop that snowball thinking and let those thoughts go.

The world, news and politics may never be free of dramas either. While it's good to be in the know, and to stand up for what you believe in, be mindful to not let everything that goes on in the outside world disrupt your inner peace, or take you off course from your own life goals and dreams.

Life can be challenging enough as it is. Be intentional to tune out drama and tune in to more peace.

*"Talk to yourself like you would
to someone you love."*
- Brené Brown

53.
Love Yourself No Matter What

My good friend Katie was $25,000 in debt and had been struggling to lose 15 pounds after her daughter was born when we met up for coffee near my apartment in the West Village.

A light snow was falling on Manhattan and I found comfort in an oversized mug of tea as my friend shared with me her struggles with money and unwanted weight. Katie told me how hard it was to feel good about herself when all she could think about was her pile of debt and not being able to fit into any of her old clothes. As I listened to my beautiful friend feeling so down on herself, all I wanted was for her to love and appreciate herself as much as the rest of us did. And to see how amazing she was as a mom, friend and overall human.

I had just finished reading *You Can Heal Your Life* by Louise Hay for the second time and was high on positivity and self-love, so I shared with Katie an exercise from the book I thought may help.

"You look in the mirror and say, 'I love and approve of myself,'" I told her. "That's it!"

Katie appreciated my support, but wasn't feeling the exercise. I understood. Truth be told, the first time I looked in the mirror and did it I felt like I was going to throw up. I kept looking over my shoulder to make sure no one would hear me, even though my two cats were the only ones living with me. It felt silly and part of me was embarrassed to say "I love myself" – like I was being full of myself. I also felt like a big-fat liar.

It took forcing myself to repeat the exercise every single day for weeks to really get the value of saying "I love you. I approve of you." And how sad is it that so many of us don't love who we are, or that we feel full of ourselves if we do?

Even just thinking about saying, "I love and approve of myself" made Katie break down in tears right there in the café.

"When I get off my butt and finally lose this weight and get my finances in order *then* I'll be able to say 'I love you' to myself." She laughed as she wiped away a tear.

I got what Katie was saying, but I encouraged her to give it a shot anyway. I'd seen firsthand that if you approach change with love, amazing transformation can take place, sometimes without much effort. I had a hunch Katie's challenges would abate once she began telling herself "I love you," and focusing on all of the things that she really *did* love about herself, versus constantly beating herself up. Because nothing good ever comes from bashing yourself.

A few hours later, I was making my way down to Soho when Katie called. She'd just done the exercise and was feeling funny about it, but told me, "What the heck?"

Three months later Katie was back in her pre-pregnancy jeans. Ten months after that she was completely out of debt. Katie still looks in the mirror every single morning and says, "I love and approve of myself."

It can feel challenging to love yourself when there are things you don't exactly *like* about yourself. But you have to do it anyway. Because when you love yourself (including anything you consider a flaw), you come to embrace, or at the very least accept, those things you don't care for. It also helps you change them with far more ease. Often, when we increase love for ourselves, we simply stop noticing something we once considered a flaw altogether.

Start building more love for yourself by giving more attention to the things you *do like, are proud of, and are working* for you. Instead of giving attention to your "wrongs," focus on everything that's *right* about you. You don't have to change what you don't like about yourself in order to love yourself, but when you increase love for yourself, you can't help but change.

Let's repeat this because understanding it will change your whole life …

You don't have to change in order to love yourself, but when you increase love for yourself, you can't help but change.

It's courageous and admirable to strive to be a better version of yourself – just remember to love the person you are in the process. We're all works in progress, gradually progressing, so love yourself fully right now. Love yourself no matter what.

54.
Step Away From Self-Blame

"I shouldn't have said that."

"I should have known better."

"I only have myself to blame."

Have you ever noticed how easy it is to make ourselves wrong? It doesn't matter if you forget to buy paper towels at the store, are turned down for a job, or someone completely does you dirty; many of us are programmed to blame ourselves for everything under the sun.

Whether it's a simple mistake we never deserved to punish ourselves for to begin with, or something completely out of our control, too often we beat ourselves up for not knowing better or *being* better and torture ourselves with "shoulda, woulda, coulda's," knowing full well it's doing us no good.

The other day my friend called me in tears after her purse was stolen from her cart at the grocery store.

"It's my fault." Her shaking voice said into the phone. "I shouldn't have walked over to the other aisle and left my purse sitting there. I never should have been so stupid!"

"Umm, no." I told her, "Whoever took your purse shouldn't have been such an asshole to steal it in the first place. Period."

It might sound crazy to you that my friend was blaming herself for someone else's wrongdoing, but chances are you've done it too. When someone takes advantage, it's easy to go into self-blame. That's why it's important to cement into your head that it's not your fault. No matter what.

It's important to own up and take responsibility for our wrongs in life and to say "I'm sorry," but it's not healthy to blame ourselves for harmless mistakes, or for things people do to take advantage of us. Even our big mistakes deserve self-forgiveness in order to allow us to show up in this world even better than before.

If years or decades ago, you chose a life path that you now know didn't serve you, it can be easy to feel regret, and even shame or self-hatred. But what's done is done and you can't go back – but you can and must move forward.

Self-blaming and shaming erodes our self-esteem, self-confidence and sense of self-worth. It can also give your power away to people who don't deserve control over your well-being.

The next time you find yourself entering self-blame territory, remind yourself, "It's not my fault."

Go on, free yourself.

55.
Be Proud of Yourself

Most of us weren't born with superhero levels of self-confidence, and a bad day at work, an argument with your teenager, or seeing something online can take a toll. Often, it seems like one thing goes wrong and then another, and suddenly you don't feel so great about yourself or your life.

For those days when you feel like you're not good enough or doing enough, cut yourself some slack and remember you're doing the best you can. Congratulate yourself on all that you do each day and take a stroll down memory lane to remind yourself of everything you've achieved so far in your life. Certainly, you've accomplished some incredible things over the years. Maybe you climbed a mountain, became a manager, or had a baby.

Give yourself a pat on the back for who you are, what you've learned and for all of the ways you've grown.

Be proud of yourself and keep in mind all of the extraordinary ways you contribute to the people you love and to the world every single day.

"All that counts in life is intention."
- Andrea Bocelli

56.
Set Intentions in Your Day

Setting intentions gives our mind direction. We decide what we want and declare it.

I fell in love with setting intentions when I was shopping for a car shortly after returning to my hometown in California after living in New York. My sweet but sleepy town lacked the ease of being able to walk to so many places, or hop on the subway, like I'd come to appreciate about Manhattan.

At first, the idea of shopping for a car excited me, but halfway through day one I took it all back. And after a few not-so-fun experiences with sales reps, I was deflating fast.

One morning, I woke up ready to see my new car in the driveway. Right then, I set an intention telling my mom, "I'm going to buy a car from someone who doesn't pressure me, someone who treats me like an old friend."

Later that day, I wandered through another car lot and heard my name being called. I turned around to see an old friend from growing up waving wildly as he ran toward me—all dressed up in his salesman attire. And from the moment we said "hello" to the moment I drove off the lot in my new car a few hours later, the whole experience was easygoing and, dare I say, fun. Not only did I buy a car from a person who treated me like an old friend like I intended, I bought it from someone who actually was an old friend.

Setting intentions creates a connection with what you want to experience. It activates the reticular activating system (RAS), a bunch of nerves sitting at the bottom of your brain that help you see what you want to see. Setting intentions is easy, painless and you can do it for anything you want, or for any part of your day.

You can intend to:

- Have a good conversation when your phone rings.
- Resolve a tech issue stress-free.
- Make your flight on time.
- Find a good parking spot.
- Learn what you need for your life right now.
- Meet new good friends.
- Have fun at the party.
- Have a brilliant idea.
- Find what you're looking for at the grocery store.
- Have a safe and easy drive from here to there.
- Laugh more. Feel better. Love yourself no matter what.

Set intentions in your head, say them out loud or write them on Post-its and place them where you'll see them. It may sound silly, or too good to be true, but give it a shot. Intend for something specific, or for something even better than you can imagine – you may be amazed by what happens!

"The first wealth is health."
- Ralph Waldo Emerson

57.
Take Good Care of Your Health

"You should be dead." My naturopath told me over the phone as we combed through my latest lab reports.

Sounds about right, I thought. I felt dead.

"This is the lowest functioning thyroid I've seen in my entire time practicing medicine." My general practitioner said to me a few hours later. "It's hardly functioning!"

Awesome, I thought.

I learned the importance of taking good care of my health the hard way – by *not* doing it. Up until this moment in my life, I was all work hard, play hard. A big morning workout followed by 10 plus hour workdays, followed by evenings out on the town was the norm. I love sleep and barely skimped on it, but the hours I was awake I moved at full speed.

My inevitable crash came hard, a few days after my beloved Grandma Nonie passed away, and I could hardly drag myself out of bed.

I'd been shuffling back and forth for a few months, working a full day and then going to visit my Nonie as she was ailing, taking advantage of every minute with her playing Bingo at the nursing home and giving back to her all of the love she gave to me and all of our family throughout her entire life.

I was honored to be with my Nonie in her last days, hours, and even breaths, especially to receive her last big smile. But saying goodbye is never easy. Especially to someone you love so deeply. It broke my heart in ways I couldn't have known how to prepare for.

Exhaustion holds hands with grief, but I'd known in my bones for quite some time that something wasn't right. I'd just pressed mute on my inner voice begging me to slow down, take time off and make an appointment with my doctor to get everything checked out.

The first diagnosis was extreme hypothyroidism. Then too, my Vitamin D, Ferritin, adrenals and a bunch of other things were in the red. Now it made sense why I was the most exhausted and physically weak version of myself I'd ever known. And why in only months I'd added 15 pounds to my petite frame, felt extreme brain fog and had debilitating anxiety that was so bad some days I couldn't leave the house alone.

If you've ever been through a health crisis, I don't have to tell you how scary and daunting it can be. Fortunately, I connected with a wonderful endocrinologist (and all-around good human) who got to the root of my health issues and re-diagnosed me with Hashimoto's, a common autoimmune disorder and the most common cause of a low-functioning thyroid. My endocrinologist wasn't just about putting a bandage on things, she was about rebalancing my whole body, boosting my immune system and restoring healthy habits. I got advice on what I should eat, what supplements to take and the importance of self-care.

I began regular acupuncture, massage therapy and sessions with a holistic nutritionist. I learned the importance of being kind to my mind and upped my "once in a while" meditation practice to every single morning. I cut back on my news and social media consumption, swapped drama TV for comedy and whenever I had an impulse to anxiously reach for my phone to Google something about my health, I gently reminded myself, "There's no need to scare myself – I will Google with care."

Instead of worrying and letting my thoughts run wild, I affirmed to myself daily:

My body is healthy, strong and resilient. I am healing more and more each day.

Healing is a journey, and it took almost six months for my body to get in balance and a few more months until I was 100% back to myself—an upgraded, healthier, and happier version of me.

Even though that time in my life was full of dark days and challenges, physically, emotionally, spiritually, and can't forget, financially, it was also the teacher I needed to truly understand that we are nothing without good health. We also have more control over how we care for our bodies, minds and spirits than we may realize.

With so much on our plates, it's easy to let our bodies take the brunt of it. We skimp on sleep, guzzle caffeine, eat on the go, pass on relaxing and spend hours sitting in front of a computer screen. It isn't until the universe gives us some kind of intervention, by the likes of an illness, sprained ankle or mental health crisis, that we're forced to pause and remember we're nothing without good health.

As you go about your day, listen to your body, mind and soul, and give them what they need. Prioritize your well-being, practice serious self-care and make it a point to:

- Honor sleep and get good rest.
- Hydrate and drink lots of water.
- Fuel your body with nourishing foods.
- Take walks, stretch out on a yoga mat and exercise for your body and mind.
- Schedule time for relaxation in your daily calendar and leave after-hours work behind.
- Go easy on stimulants like coffee and sugary drinks.
- Practice moderation with alcohol, it may seem like it brings you up, but it actually acts as a depressant.
- Meditate and be kind to your mind.
- Choose laughter, entertainment, activities and people who make you feel good.

- Pay attention to how you feel and if something in your body feels off, seek help. Don't push it back or delay, and always get a second opinion if you're not satisfied with the first.
- Be your strongest health advocate, because while doctors, naturopaths and specialists mean well and will do their best to help, no one knows your body like you do.
- Practice positive self-talk and remind yourself that you are healthy, strong and resilient.

Take good care of yourself so you can give the world the absolute best of you – not what's barely left of you.

58.
Prioritize Sleep

The list of things we can live without is long, but good sleep isn't one of them. Our bodies heal when we sleep and we need quality zzz's to restore and recharge. Sleep is essential, and not enough can leave us more susceptible to colds, flus, brain fog and mental overwhelm. It can also make us grumpy and not much fun to be around!

Many of us go to bed *only after* everything on our to-do list has been taken care of. But good slumber actually *increases* productivity, and not getting enough can make your daily tasks more challenging because you're dragging.

Make getting a good night's sleep a priority by creating a hard-stop for using your phone an hour or two before bedtime. This means you don't check email, social media or reply to texts. Let your mind unwind by doing something relaxing, like taking a warm shower or bath, reading a book or sipping chamomile tea. Bedtime routines work wonders for babies *and* adults and each step will signal to your brain that it's getting time to say goodnight.

If during the day you feel a dip in energy or catch yourself nodding off, give yourself permission to lie down and take a 10 or 20-minute nap. A little siesta can restore alertness, improve memory, productivity, reduce stress, improve mood ... plus it feels great!

Depending on where you live in the world, an afternoon nap may be as common as a morning espresso. Naps are taken without guilt or feeling the need to down a cup of coffee and shake it off. If you feel tired, you simply lay down. But in many cultures, napping as an adult can be frowned upon or deemed lazy (unless you're on vacation or finished off the turkey at Thanksgiving!). But napping didn't stop Thomas Edison, Leonardo da Vinci, Winston Churchill, Eleanor Roosevelt, Albert Einstein, John F. Kennedy, Bill Clinton, Margaret Thatcher and numerous other famous nappers from inventing electricity, painting masterpieces, running countries and changing the world.

You know how great it feels to be rested, so make quality sleep a priority in your life and enjoy waking up feeling refreshed.

59.
Move Your Body and Exercise

Exercise is good for our bodies, minds and souls. It helps keep our hearts healthy, our lungs breathing deeply, our immune system strong and our bodies in good physical shape.

Exercise clears our minds and helps us tap into our creative side. We often work out inner struggles and find solutions to problems when we're in motion. Plus, we release endorphins when we exercise and can enjoy a satisfying high!

With everything on the calendar, it's easy to let exercise slip off the schedule, so it's important to make it part of your daily lifestyle. There's no need to set aside an hour to go to the gym every day – a morning or evening walk in nature or 10 minutes of gentle yoga or stretching can do wonders. Even a set of push-ups, sit-ups and lunges while waiting for your coffee to brew will give your body a boost.

Find exercise that makes sense for your life and enjoy it. Once you realize how good it feels, it's easy for exercise to become the highlight of your day.

60.
Be Kind to Your Mind and Meditate

We all know how important it is to take good care of our bodies. We read nutrition labels, buy organic when we can, and exercise with care, knowing our bodies will thank us for it. But how often do you consider how you treat your mind?

Most of us take in so much mentally from reading the news, scrolling social media, talking with friends and neighbors, binging TV series, and even overhearing strangers chatting in line at the grocery store. But mentally consuming so much in a day can make the happiest of us feel blue, the most energized feel depleted and the most hopeful fear the worst. And too much outer noise can cause inner chaos in anyone.

Designate time in your day to let your mind rest. The kindest thing you can do is to meditate. Even just 15 or 20 minutes does wonders for your mind and can lower your heart rate, reduce stress and help you sleep soundly.

If you're new to meditation, ask a friend who practices for advice or search online for guided meditations that walk you through how it's done. And if you're short on time, simply sit and take a few big breaths in, letting your belly expand. Hold for a second or two, then slowly exhale. Be still, take your time and let your mind enjoy some calm.

*"A good laugh and a long sleep are
the two best cures for anything."*
- Irish Proverb

61.
Laugh, a Lot

Laughing is fun and good for your health. Giving a little chuckle or laughing 'till you cry boosts your immune system, relieves pain, lessens depression and even helps your heart. Plus, having a good laugh just feels so good!

Seek out laughter in your day. Find time to be goofy with your kids and pets, play games, watch funny TV shows and movies, and surround yourself with people who like to laugh, too.

Life can be stressful and oh-so-serious, but we can make it a whole lot easier by approaching things with a sense of humor. Have you ever returned home from the grocery store and realized you forgot the *one thing* you went there to get? Or, have you insisted something was true, only to find out that it wasn't?

We all do some pretty funny things, whether we mean to or not. Instead of being hard on yourself, be light, embrace your "whoops!" moments and laugh them off.

Remember, if you can't change or fix something in life, try to find a way to laugh with it.

62.
Scroll Social Media With Care

Many of us have a love/hate relationship with social media. We love how it helps us stay in touch with far-away friends and family, and brings attention to work, good causes and social projects. But we also know it can suck us in, take us off purpose and affect our moods more than we'd like to admit.

It's hard to know what you'll get when you hop on social media. Will you smile or burst into laughter? Hopefully. Will something get under your skin and make you feel annoyed or upset? Perhaps. Will you feel insecure, left out, or worse off than you did before going on? Unfortunately, there's a chance you will. It's not uncommon to get a full emotional roller coaster ride in one quick scroll. In 30 seconds you might see a hilarious post of your friend's puppy, a political rant from an old co-worker, and a former classmates' montage of her perfect family vacation.

If social media is a part of your life, be intentional to protect your mental well-being by approaching it in a mind-kind way. Know that spending hours combing through an ex-partner or an ex-friend's photos, or obsessing over someone else's seemingly perfect life can be downright damaging, emotionally.

Out of sight, out of mind is real, and unlike co-workers, neighbors or in-laws, you get to choose your social media people and there's no need to follow anyone who brings you down or who isn't in your real life for a reason. If seeing someone's posts or comments stirs up bad memories, or makes you feel anything but good, prioritize your happiness and disconnect from them.

Unlike work, a good book, TV series, or the stock market, social media never pauses and it never ends, so it's up to you to create healthy boundaries with it. Instead of hopping on whenever you have a few minutes to spare, schedule a block of time to engage once or twice daily and set a timer for 10 minutes so you don't get sucked in. Give your brain and nervous system a break by staying off completely for the first two and last three hours of your day.

Pay attention to how social media makes you feel and after going on, be sure to ask yourself, "Am I happier now than I was before?" If the answer is "no" too often, you might want to take an extended break, or ditch the digital chatter completely.

"If you're not able to sit down and do nothing for 1 hour, you're addicted to stimulation, and you will never attain true happiness."
- Robert Celner

63.
Put Down Your Phone

Phone addiction is real, and chances are you spend a lot of time reaching for that little device for no apparent reason. While all of the apps and gadgets are a blessing in many ways, our minds can easily get overstimulated and overwhelmed. Plus, our necks and shoulders take on a lot when we're constantly looking down.

It's hard to disconnect when you are glued to your tech, but be aware of your relationship with your phone and try to break the habit of reaching for it so much. When you have a few extra minutes on your hands, instead of looking down, look up and see what's going on right in front of you. If you're waiting for a friend to arrive at a restaurant, enjoy real life interaction and strike up a conversation with your server or a fellow customer instead of hopping on an app. When you're taking a rideshare, stare out the window, take in the scenery and allow your mind to wander, rather than texting someone. Instead of asking your phone for an immediate answer to a question, give your brain some exercise and let it think for a minute.

Like caramel fudge ice cream, binging bad TV, or chilled margaritas on a hot summer day, too much of a good thing can easily turn into a bad thing. There's a point when you have to say "that's enough" and take back control of your time.

Remember, you are in charge of your phone, not the other way around.

"We have two ears and one mouth so we can listen twice as much as we speak."
- Epictetus

64.
Be a Better Listener

How often do you find yourself in a conversation, but not really listening to what the other person is saying? Maybe you're nodding your head and smiling, but thinking about what you're going to say next, or waiting for a pause to jump in with your own two cents. Maybe too, you are secretly (or quite obviously!) stealing glances at your phone.

Lately, it seems that more and more people aren't *really* listening to each other, or at least not slowing down and taking in what the other person is saying. We can be so staunch in our own views that we simply don't pay attention to those who we don't see eye-to-eye with. Instead, we tune out, telling ourselves, "Sigh, whatever … I'm right, they're wrong, end of story!" Having our phones always within reach hasn't helped. They ping and light up, and even a quick look takes us out of the present.

While it's totally OK to disagree, if we're too quick to shut someone down, we miss out on the chance to hear where they're coming from. If we let down our guard, we can open ourselves up to see things from another person's perspective, and open the door for them to understand why we see things how *we* do. When we loosen our grip, we create space to learn from one another.

People love feeling heard, so give yourself and the people you are talking with the gift of being a good listener. Keep your phone tucked away and your mind open. When it's your turn to talk, speak clearly and gently. It's impossible to listen to someone who is yelling, and no one appreciates being talked down to. Do your best to communicate respectfully so you can be truly heard – and others will likely follow your tone.

"What you think, you become. What you feel, you attract. What you imagine, you create."
- Buddha

65.
Practice Affirmations

Muhammad Ali is widely considered the greatest heavyweight-boxing champion in history. But long before he was actually a champ, he'd affirm: "Float like a butterfly, sting like a bee. Nobody can beat, Muhammad Ali!"

Ali understood the power of his thoughts and words and how to use affirmations to create the life he wanted. "It's the repetition of affirmations that leads to belief." Ali said, "And once that belief becomes a deep conviction, things begin to happen."

We were all raised with certain beliefs about life. Whether we learned them from family, friends, faith or teachers, or through observations and experiences, we've collected beliefs about money, love, work, health, sex, culture and most everything we know. Often, unbeknownst to us, we've decided certain ways of living are right, wrong, bad, good, true, false.

The interesting thing about beliefs is that except for a few (like the world being flat!), most are only true if we believe them to be. For example, if you grew up seeing divorce happening all around you, you may have a belief that even the best relationships eventually come to an end. If someone told you money only came with struggle and sacrifice, or you witnessed that growing up, you may hold a belief about money that it's hard to come by.

A belief may be true for you, but it doesn't mean it's true for someone else.

Why does this matter? Because our lives often mirror our beliefs and we get more of what we believe to be true – whether we want to or not.

Take my friends Mike and Billy for example. Mike's never had any issues or hang-ups about money. He was raised to go to school, get a job and put 10% of his paycheck into savings and give 10% to charity. He's always believed that money is available and is happy to have it and share it. Billy, on the other hand, grew up in a household where money was scarce and there were no guarantees it would show up – no matter how hard you worked.

I spoke with both Mike and Billy the other day and in less than the 30 minutes Mike and I were on the phone, he came across an abandoned $20 bill in a parking lot. Go figure! On the flip side of the beliefs coin, when I talked to Billy, he'd just learned that the raise he was promised six months ago wouldn't arrive for another few months. Both situations only reconfirmed their already formed beliefs about money.

The good news about beliefs is they can be changed. According to author Abraham Hicks, a belief is just a thought you keep thinking over and over. So, how do we change our beliefs so we can improve our lives? We change our thinking by practicing affirmations.

Affirmations are powerful statements declaring something to be true. We can use affirmations to program (or re-program!) our minds to create beliefs that serve us. If this sounds a bit too woo-woo, let's go back to what Muhammad Ali said: "It's the repetition of affirmations that leads to belief. And once that belief becomes a deep conviction, things begin to happen."

Working with affirmations is so easy it can feel too good to be true. But take it from Muhammad Ali – they're packed with a powerful punch and really do work!

If there's something in your life you want to change, or experience, first ask yourself the tough questions and find out if any beliefs are standing in your way. Chances are, you heard, observed or experienced something that caused you to believe that's how things go. Gather the information so you can make the improvements you want to see in your life.

Next, create a statement affirming what you want to be true.

For example, if you want to feel more confident, you may affirm: "I am beautiful. I am smart. I am kind. I am wonderful. People love and appreciate me fully."

If you want to have more money, you may affirm: "I am worthy and deserving of money. My income is constantly increasing. Money always shows up and I always have more than enough."

If you want to be in a loving relationship, you may affirm: "I am in a happy and healthy relationship with a wonderful, loving partner. I am worthy and deserving of love."

If you want to improve your health, you may affirm: "My body is healthy, strong, and resilient. I am healing more and more each day." (This affirmation worked wonders for me.)

Once you decide on your affirmations, commit to practicing them daily. I find taking a few minutes in the morning to write them down 10-20 times to be especially powerful.

It's completely normal when you first begin to feel like this practice is a joke. If you're fresh out of a break-up, or have debt collectors calling, it's going to feel phony to tell yourself, "I'm always lucky in love." Or, "I have more than enough money."

Do it anyway.

Changing a belief using affirmations is like learning a new language or training for a marathon. It won't happen overnight. That's why repeating them daily is crucial. The more you repeat your affirmations, the more you'll begin believing them. In time your body will feel strong, like "of course this is true for me!" and your voice will have conviction. (And it *can* take time, so be patient.) Once you believe something to be true and you feel it strongly in your bones, you'll start seeing those positive changes reflected in your life.

Now, is affirming enough? Maybe. But Muhammad Ali wouldn't have become the champ he was if he didn't spend hours training at the gym and ultimately jump into the ring. But even with all the training in the world, Ali knew that in order to be the best, he first had to *believe* he was.

Our words have a powerful impact on our lives and while affirmations may sound too easy, or good to be true, they're known for making magic happen. At the very least, tell yourself on repeat that life is on your side and things are going your way.

Affirmations for your life:

"I am beautiful, smart, kind and wonderful."

"My body is healthy, strong and resilient."

"I always have more than enough money."

"I am in a healthy, happy, loving relationship."

"Life loves and supports me." (Louise Hay)

"Everything is always working out for me." (Abraham Hicks)

*"You don't have to set yourself
on fire to keep others warm."*
- Unknown

66.
Create Healthy Boundaries

Most of us are good people and enjoy making others happy. We like saying "yes" to what people ask of us and overall try to be agreeable. (After all, we're human and want to be helpful and liked!). So it can feel natural to drop what we are doing, lose sleep, and turn our schedules upside down to accommodate others.

The problem? Sometimes when we say "yes," especially to the same people again and again, we find ourselves doing things that don't actually work for us, bending over backwards, and ultimately feeling resentment, regret, and even taken advantage of. Sometimes, we give so much that our lives become imbalanced and we start feeling exhausted, falling short on our own goals and even sick from burnout.

There will always be times when someone needs us more, and vice versa. That's part of life and relationships. But, if you're constantly giving, or feeling like someone is asking too much of you, or if you find yourself always bending to do what's best for someone else rather than what's best for you, it's time to set some healthy boundaries.

Be honest, when was the last time you set boundaries in your life?

If your answer is, "it's been a while," or "I'm not sure I actually *ever* have" you are not alone. Setting boundaries can seem uncomfortable because it often involves saying "no" and risks disappointing people. But like author and speaker Brené Brown says, "Daring to set boundaries is about having the courage to love ourselves even when we risk disappointing others."

I'm an early riser, so I rarely take a phone call after 8 p.m. so I can get into sleep mode. This is a boundary I've set for myself so I don't wake up feeling exhausted and regret taking that late-night call. My friends know that if they want to have a lengthy convo with me, we have to start earlier. I love chatting with my friends, but this is a boundary I set for myself to get good rest and to feel my best.

My Grandma Nonie was hands-down the kindest and most generous person on the planet. She gave so much to everyone she loved and in her early 90's she really started prioritizing her own needs too, especially her limits and when she'd had enough. "That's enough," she'd say in her sweet voice and put down her fork in the middle of dinner, knowing her stomach didn't need anything more – even if it meant she didn't finish the delicious meal my mom made. "That's enough," she'd say and get up during a conversation to go take a lie-down if her body needed rest – even if someone was in mid-speech. "That's enough," she said at the dining table at her nursing home and smiled as she dug into her dinner when a priest was still giving a pre-meal blessing. (In truth, the blessing was running long and the food was getting cold!)

We create boundaries not to hurt others, but to love ourselves more.

Starting now, put yourself at the head of your receiving line and set healthy boundaries with friends, loved ones, work and even with yourself. If you feel overwhelmed or you need a break, let your phone ring to voicemail. Learn to be OK with letting an hour, or even a few days pass by before replying to non-urgent emails and texts. And most important, get comfortable saying, "No." For some reason many of us feel "No" must be accompanied by a reason – a better, more important reason. But just so you know, "No" is a complete sentence and there *is no* better or more important reason than to take care of yourself. You don't have to create an elaborate excuse or over explain yourself when you set boundaries. "I'm sorry, but I won't be able to" or "Another time will be better" or simply "No" really *is* enough. The right people will get it and respect your wishes. And if someone tries to push, manipulate or make you feel guilty, it's further proof you're doing the right thing and that boundaries are in order. And probably overdue!

> We create boundaries not to hurt others, but to love ourselves more.

We tend to think we're the center of the universe and if we don't show up the world will collapse, but thankfully it's not true. Our friends, family, neighbors, co-workers and everyone will be just fine. The show will go on without us.

Boundaries are an act of self-care, so consider them a much deserved gift to yourself. And remember, the happier you are the happier everyone around you will be, too.

67.
Try Not to Take Things Personally

"Did I do something wrong?" We think when someone is short with us.

"Are they upset with me?" We wonder if someone doesn't call us back right away.

When things like this happen, our minds run wild with stories and we often take what other people say or do personally. But it's important to remember that their behavior isn't about us, it's about them.

We've all felt ignored by someone only to later find out they didn't return our call because their phone died, or they were going through a stressful time. Chances are you've been on the other side and seen an acquaintance walking down the grocery store aisle or across a parking lot, and you pretended not to see them. Most likely it wasn't because you don't like the person, but you weren't in the mood for small talk, or you were in a hurry, or even having a bad hair day. Your ignoring them had nothing to do with them personally, it was about you.

If you've ever loved an alcoholic or an addict, there's a good chance at some point you realized that their evasive behavior, broken promises or elaborate lies, while they may have hurt like hell, had nothing to do with you. It was their addiction running the show.

Other people's thoughts, behavior and actions are a reflection of them, not you. Instead of questioning yourself when your boss or rideshare driver is rude, or someone's taking a while to get back to you, shrug it off knowing it's not about you. They have other things going on in their lives and you may even bring out their own insecurities or jealousies, which is also about them, not you. And if you ever do want to know if something is up, find the courage to ask the tough questions and get clarification. Most likely, the person will shower you with apologies, saying their behavior wasn't personal and had nothing to do with you.

"Don't confuse activity with productivity. Many people are simply busy at being busy."
- Robin Sharma

68.
Schedule Your Day in a More Productive Way

Some days fly by and in what feels like a blink – it's already time to make dinner. "Where did the time go?" You ask yourself. We may not get as much done as we'd like to in most days, but there *are* ways to maximize the hours and to be more productive:

Create a pre-day agenda

You save time and brain power when you wake up already knowing the game-plan for the day. So, each evening, take five minutes to write down your plans for the next day. Put a star next to anything that must get done in that 24-hour window. Schedule your tasks in an order that makes the most sense to save time.

Unexpected things do come up, and open space in your calendar allows you to breathe easier and enjoy more, so if the day looks crammed, be intentional to eliminate, outsource or move things to another day. Be realistic about how much you take on.

There's nothing fun about getting to the end of a full day and feeling bad for not doing all that you set out to do.

Focus on your most important projects first

We tend to have more energy and focus earlier in the day, so tackle what's necessary to move the needle toward your current goals first. Remember, create for yourself before you consume from others – this way, no matter what comes up you'll know you accomplished something important to you in this life season.

Give tasks your undivided attention

Some people take pride in multitasking, but it can actually slow us down and take us off purpose. Be present with what's right in front of you and give each task your full attention. Set an alarm for 30, 50 or 90 minutes to help you focus on nothing else until the alarm rings.

Make fewer decisions

We make dozens of decisions in a day: what to wear, what to eat, when to exercise, what TV show to watch, etc. While the choices may be minor, together they consume a ton of mental energy and can lead to decision fatigue. (This is why, at the end of the day, it can be so hard to decide what to eat for dinner or to watch on TV!)

Eliminate decisions by sticking to a routine when you can. Jeans and a blouse for a go-to outfit? Salad or a sandwich for lunch? Early evening walk?

Use free time on the weekends to decide on dinners for the week, and add TV shows and movies to your queue to watch so you don't find yourself at the end of a long weekday spending hours watching trailers.

Take the path of least resistance when you find yourself overthinking and confusing yourself regarding a decision. What feels lightest to you? What will be easiest?

There's a certain satisfaction in getting everything crossed off your to-do list, but you never want to be so exhausted at the end of the day that you ruin the next day before it begins. Most weeks are marathons, not sprints, so reserve energy for tomorrow and make room in your evenings to relax and recharge.

69.
Ask for Help

"I can do it myself!" According to my parents, this was one of my go-to phrases as a child.

Fiercely independent? *Check.* ✓

Wanting things done how I wanted them done? *Check, Check.* ✓✓

Not comfortable being vulnerable and asking for help? *Check. Check. Check.* ✓✓✓

Asking for help can be hard, even when we truly want it. Sometimes we're too proud, or we don't want to put anyone out. Other times, it's a trust factor and we don't think anyone will do the job as well as we will. Or, we've become so used to doing things on our own that we don't even think to ask. But nothing good comes from feeling stressed or overwhelmed and we all can use a helping hand from time to time.

Take note of where you can benefit from help in your days, then go ahead and ask for it. Even when we think it's obvious we may be hinting for help from those around us, people aren't mind readers and you really do have to come right out and ask.

While we are amazing and can do a million things all by ourselves, we really don't need to. When your calendar is overflowing, call on family and friends or hire someone, and let yourself be helped. If you're nervous it won't be done as well as when you do it, keep an open mind. You may be surprised to find out another way is just as good – or even better. At the very least, be grateful for the time and mental space it frees up for you. Keep in mind how happy you are to help others, and know that they'll feel good helping you, too.

Even if we can carry the load, we don't need to overextend ourselves, so lower your guard, be vulnerable and ask for help.

"To live a fulfilled life, we need to keep creating the 'what is next' of our lives."
- Mark Twain

70.
Try Something New

Trying something new is invigorating. Walking into a beginner's fitness class, signing up for language lessons, or attempting to cook a new meal forces you to step out of your comfort zone and spices things up. It gives you a sense of pride and accomplishment that you simply don't get when sticking to the same old, same old.

Like many things we know will be good for us, it can be challenging to break with routine, take the plunge and dive into something new. But you don't need to overthink it or make it a big deal. Simply start by writing down a handful of activities, goals, and even meals that excite you. Traveling internationally? Playing Pickleball? Taking a pottery class? Tai Chi? Gardening? Creative storytelling? Write down anything that sounds fun and then choose one to begin with and schedule it in your calendar.

You don't have to sail across the world, master the piano or learn how to cook a six-course meal to enrich your life. Just try out something new for the fun of it and don't be afraid to be a beginner.

71.
Try Not to Compare Yourself to Others

It's easy to look at friends, co-workers or fellow parents at your kid's school and compare accomplishments, relationships, vacations, how kind, relaxed or high-strung they are – even the brownies they made (or bought!). But when we make these comparisons, we tend to put ourselves down and doubt our own capabilities. We also risk unfairly judging people which creates separation.

There's always going to be someone to view as "better off" than you and also someone who isn't. So how you feel about yourself only depends on who you are comparing yourself to. And the real danger in comparing your life with others is you're not honoring who *you* are. It makes you not appreciate and love your life for what it is right now.

The next time you feel tempted to compare yourself to others or think something like, "Why can't my life be like that?"

remind yourself that no matter how great you think someone has it, you don't know the full story about anyone else's life, even your best friends.

We're all on our own journey, doing life our own way, at our own speed and are exactly where we're supposed to be.

> We're all on our own journey, doing life our own way, at our own speed and are exactly where we're supposed to be.

*"The surest way to be happy is
to seek happiness for others."*
- Dr. Martin Luther King, Jr.

72.
Be Happy for People

It can be hard to feel genuine happiness for others when we're not in the best place. Even when we truly want to. Hearing about someone else's good fortune can make us feel behind, fearful good things won't happen to us and bad about where we stand in life.

But Dr. Martin Luther King, Jr. was right when he said, "The surest way to be happy is to seek happiness for others." It's time to start being happy for people and not only because it's the right thing to do and you want to be, deep down. But doing so will actually boost your own good fortune too. After all, birds of a feather flock together.

The next time someone lets you know of their happy news, especially if it's something you want for your life too, instead of feeling sorry for yourself or angry at life because "it's not fair," talk to them about their promotion, new home, world travels or baby on the way. Bask in their grateful energy and you'll find yourself feeling genuinely happy for them and excited for it to happen to you too. Because if they can experience this great fortune, well, then so can you!

73.
Plant Good Seeds for Others

It doesn't always feel like it, but people really do listen to what we say. That's why one of the kindest things you can do for another human being is to do what I call "Plant Good Seeds."

To Plant Good Seeds means to give your friends, family and everyone around you optimism, belief in themselves and hope. If a friend is frustrated over finding a job after a layoff, instead of saying things like, "It's nearly impossible to find anything good," plant a good seed by reminding them how wonderful they are and how many amazing companies would love to hire them (because it's true!). If your daughter wants to do something no woman has ever done before, tell her she can do what she puts her heart and mind to and to go blaze a trail.

Planting good seeds isn't about giving unauthentic advice or placating someone. You can still be straightforward and realistic with people while also being optimistic. When someone is standing on an emotional ledge, the last thing you want to do is say something that will make them jump. When you share positive stories that remind them of possibilities, you activate a thought in their mind that plants a seed of belief. So why not make it a hopeful one?

74.
Be Part of Something

The world can get lonely, and it's important to put yourself out there to create community and join groups, organizations, classes and clubs. Not only does being part of something connect you with new friends who share a common interest, it gives you that sense of connection and belonging we all need.

Whether it's a regular gathering with like-minded people in a book or wine tasting club, writer's group, volunteer organization, or entrepreneur mastermind, make it a point to be a part of something. Even becoming a local at your neighborhood coffee shop or dog park will give you a sense of community. Or a bar like Cheers where everyone knows your name!

The world is full of wonderful people, so keep an open mind when putting yourself out there. You are smart enough to spot red flags but you don't need to go into new friendships searching for them. Like Will Rogers said, "A stranger is just a friend I haven't yet met."

Keep looking until you find that place where you feel embraced.

> "We bereaved are not alone. We belong to the largest company in all the world, the company of those who have known suffering."
> - Helen Keller

75.
Grieve Your Losses

Loss is a part of life, and each and every one of us will be brought to our knees by the pain of grief. We all will experience heartbreak so deep that it takes our breath away. This is part of the human experience – no one is exempt.

When you are faced with a loss, whether it's the death of a loved one, divorce, or the loss of your home or a job you cherished and depended on, let yourself grieve, fully. Grieving is a process, and it is a time when emotions run wild, so be present with all that you feel and be patient with yourself.

One moment you may feel devastation so extreme in your bones that you may not be able to pull yourself out of bed. The next day you may see something funny, and even laugh out loud. Hearing the sound of your own laughter may feel like relief, or it could make you question how you could ever feel a sliver of joy at a time like this. You'll look out the window and see that life is still going on, even when the world as you have known it has collapsed.

Grieve your losses fully and know that you are not alone. Be gentle with yourself and talk with friends, work with therapists and go to support groups. You don't have to carry this load on your own, and having support is more important than you may realize. It can be difficult to share, but it's a healthy part of the process, even if you can't make sense of things.

Time is our greatest foe and also our friend when we're grieving. Because time heals wounds, things eventually become more bearable, even if the pain never fully subsides. The immediate aftershock can feel like a tsunami crashing into you without warning, knocking you off your feet and leaving you gasping for air. But with time, the waves of grief will become easier to ride out.

Perhaps the only gift of grief is that you can now see so clearly all that truly matters in life. Certain dramas, people or situations that only just a week before may have consumed you, now seem so insignificant. Your perspective has shifted and suddenly your life purpose and the people you love are magnified, and everything else falls away into the background. Make note of this and don't forget it.

Saying goodbye when we aren't ready to, and experiencing unwanted change is never easy. We will be shaken, shattered and temporarily robbed of our faith in life. We will feel loss permeate through every cell in our body and every fabric of our soul.

And yet, we will go on. We have no choice.

Though it may be too hard to imagine when you are in the process of grieving, with time, you will smile, laugh and love. Your life will be sweet again.

"When the storm seems to overpower you, hold tight, for it is only passing."
- Hiral Nagda

76.
Make Peace With Uncertainty

We all face uncertain times where we feel like things are up in the air. If living with more questions than answers makes you feel uneasy, you are not alone. All of the wondering and wishing for something definitive can drive you crazy, and leave you stressed, depressed or worried sick.

When outside forces are beyond your control, the best thing you can do is shift your focus to control your own personal self, including self-care, what you read, watch and listen to, and who you spend your time with. You also get to decide which thoughts you will entertain and which ones you can let go of.

To feel even a tiny bit better, try to make peace with this time in your life, surrender and allow life to guide you. Having an affirmation, mantra or a serenity prayer in your back pocket is a necessity, too. Whenever you start asking yourself a question, like, "When will I …" or "What's going to happen if …"

and you find yourself feeling scared, sad or overwhelmed, reach for positivity and assure yourself:

Everything is going to be OK.

I am not alone.

Life has a way of working out.

I am getting through this.

You are human and you're allowed to feel all that you do when life feels scary or uncertain. Go easy on yourself.

Life can change on a dime, and we can't control what we can't control. The best thing we can do for ourselves is to try and make peace with uncertainty, have faith that everything will be OK, surrender and take a deep breath.

"Change is the only constant in life."
- Heraclitus

77.
Go Easy With Life Changes

Some people get excited by change, but many of us prefer the comfort of what we already know. After all, big or small, change can make us feel vulnerable, overwhelmed and uneasy. But as difficult as the adjustment process may be, change can be a wonderful thing. Yes, moving, starting a new job, or having a baby can bring about a host of new challenges, but it also invites growth, adventures, and allows you to witness your own inner strength.

When going through a life change, help yourself transition a little smoother and:

Plan for a change before it happens

Some changes you know about well in advance. Others come as a big surprise! When you know a change is coming, do your best to plan for it ahead of time. If you're moving, don't just schedule the movers to come, but start downsizing early and prepare yourself emotionally. You may feel sad to leave your home, and know that is perfectly OK.

Schedule one change at a time

When change happens, our lives can feel rocked. And layering on multiple changes at once can make us feel anxious and overwhelmed. Do your best to take care of yourself mentally and physically and try to fully adjust to one change in your current life season before adding in another.

Go easy

Change can rock our nervous system and there's an adjustment phase that we need to recognize and go easy about. Even if you're excited about a change, like your child starting school or your own retirement, it can stir up all kinds of emotions and weigh on you. Understand that you may feel uneasy for a while. You may need more rest and sleep. You may need time to adjust to a new routine. You may need to have more patience with yourself and with others.

Allow yourself to feel everything without judgment. Talk with friends and people who support you. Lighten your load and create as much open calendar space as possible so you don't get too overwhelmed.

Welcome or not, change is a part of life, and big or small, you can handle it all.

"The most important decision we make is whether we believe we live in a friendly or hostile universe."
- Albert Einstein

78.
Choose Love Over Fear

There are two ways we approach life – through the lenses of love or fear. And life presents no shortage of opportunities for us to make decisions coming from a place of either.

When we say "yes" to a relationship or a new job we're not excited about, or we make an offer on a home or sign a lease on an apartment that doesn't feel 100% right in our bones, it's often because we are afraid nothing better will come along. Or, we feel like we are running out of time. We're operating in scarcity mode, dearth and lack – in other words, fear.

But when we make a choice rooted in love, it's as if our heart is exploding with "yeses" and we have zero doubts coursing through our veins – only the feeling of excitement or peace. It's all about abundance, possibility and pure joy.

We all have physiological and safety needs to be met, so it can be easy to feel a need to choose someone or something – even when it's not what we truly want or hoped for. The problem in doing so is that often these fear-driven decisions come back to bite us in the butt! At some point, we encounter misfortunes, setbacks, "what if's" and even face regrets for saying "yes," because in our hearts we knew it wasn't the best fit.

As you go about your day, pay attention to whether you are approaching life with love or fear. When you are moving forward in fear, usually your body will be your first indicator because it won't feel that great. Maybe you are tense or have a sinking feeling in your stomach. Maybe you feel shortness of breath or a pounding headache. You may even come down with a cold, stub your toe or get a flat tire to slow you down.

But when you choose out of love everything feels light, right, peaceful and good. You are excited, content, grateful and without reservations. It's how it should be and you know it.

It can be easy to let fear run the show, to give in to doubt and say "yes" when deep down we feel it's a "no." Even with reservations, bright red flags and heavy hearts we may move forward because we are afraid this is it – it's our only chance or choice.

Life will present you with no shortage of opportunities to make choices out of love or fear. Do your best to go with love. If you feel you *do* have to make a choice that's out of fear, lack or scarcity, make sure it's only temporary and do what you can to keep your options open.

Abundance and possibilities are all around us, and like the poet Rumi said, "Your heart knows the way. Run in that direction."

*"Be open to everything
and attached to nothing."*
- Dr. Wayne Dyer

79.
Let Life Surprise and Delight You

Growing up, my family spent much of our time on a small Hawaiian island my parents fell in love with on their honeymoon. We'd splash in the warm water, jump off secret waterfalls and chase rainbows until we fell into the soft sand. The island was the backdrop for many happy memories for our family and I felt a strong connection and a sense of belonging from the first time I stepped off the plane. One day, as I sat on the shore thanking the island for another magical visit, I looked out to the teal blue water and had a strong feeling that someday, I'd call this island home.

Fast-forward a couple of decades, and I was on a solo-cation on that same beach. As I floated in the water, a couple swam over, laughing and splashing on their honeymoon. I was happily single at the time, but something about the friendship and fun they were having made me want that too. I looked up to the sky between the fluffy golden clouds and made a wish to my Aunt Bonnie, my Nonie and Grandma Dorothy, my gal pal angels in the heavens above, and asked them to connect me with someone who would make me smile in the same way. "Next time I'm on this beach," I said, "I'd love to be hand-in-hand with a wonderful man."

A few minutes later, I settled onto my towel on the sand and my phone lit up with a text from a toxic ex. "Not him!" I shook my head looking up to my angels in the sky.

Shortly after returning home to California, I received an invite to an event hosted by an author I'd been a fan of for years. Part spiritual workshop, part big party, the event was taking place the following November in Waikiki Beach on a neighboring island of my favorite. It wasn't the right time for me to travel, but a voice inside kept saying, "You have to go."

So, I went.

The first minute of the very first evening of the event, I serendipitously met a man who, from the moment we said "hello," we both had this feeling like, "Where have you been all my life?" I'd never felt such a strong connection or so at ease with anyone so instantly.

He'd been living on my favorite island for the past 15 years and only 10 minutes from the beach I'd spent so much time on as a child. We even had friends of friends in common.

Our first date lasted 10 days. It started with an early morning walk with coffee on the beach before one of our workshops, and ended with me flying back home with him to my favorite island.

Our plane touched down at 8 p.m. in the middle of a torrential downpour. We ran to his car and between the pitch-black night and wild wind and rain it was hard to even tell where we were. But by the time day broke the next morning, the storm had passed. The island was still.

"Want to grab coffee and watch the sunrise on the beach?" he asked.

"Absolutely!" I said.

A few minutes later, we were walking hand-in-hand in the sand. It felt good to be back on the island. The ocean and air felt so alive. And a few minutes after that, we turned a corner, climbed over some rocks and what lay in front of me took my breath away. We were in the exact spot I'd made my wish to my late Aunt Bonnie and my grandmas, my angels, only a year before. Standing there together, just like I'd asked for.

I never imagined connecting with a wonderful man would have unfolded how it did – it was all so easy and natural. It was how it was supposed to be, and I knew it. Even better, it was playing out in one of my happiest places in the world.

I realized right then how important it is to say "yes" to where life calls you – even when it doesn't make sense or seem like the right time – and to stay willing to go with the flow.

I looked down at our hands interlocked in love and then up at the sky to my angels. "Thank you."

80.
Be Open to Life's Possibilities

Eighteen months after walking on the beach that morning with my new love, my hunch as a child that I'd someday call the island home turned out to be right.

After my dog, Harper, and I settled into our beautiful new home just a short walk from that special shore, we became regulars on a hiking trail that spans miles above the Pacific Ocean. The trail has many different pathways you can venture on, and if you get there early enough in the morning you can watch the sunrise over the water, and during certain times of the year in the evening, you can see it set back into the sea.

One day, I took my mom on the trail to show her my favorite lookout point. As we soaked in the tranquil colors of the ocean, a woman slightly out of breath approached us.

"Aloha," she said, and my mom and I could tell she was distressed. "Do you know how to get back to the beach? I seem to have gotten lost from the path."

My mom and I were on no schedule, so we took our time walking the woman through the trees and sandy terrain, down a path that led back to the beach. And a few minutes later she let out a huge sigh of relief when she touched the shore.

"It's a good thing you know your way around here," my mom said as we resumed our hike back up the cliff. "That woman seemed scared she wouldn't find the right way back."

I paused at the top and pointed to dozens of sandy pathways leading in and out of the scattered trees surrounding us. "There is no right way, mom," I told her. "Any of these paths would've taken the woman back to the beach. She just panicked because she thought there was *only one way*, and she couldn't figure out which one it was."

Life is a lot like that cliff – it's full of different paths and possibilities. There is no one right way to something we want, there are several ways. But like the woman my mom and I encountered that day, often we get tripped up when we fear we took a wrong turn, made a mistake, or strayed from the perfect course.

It's tempting to try and control every single thing, but when we hold too tight to the wheel and find ourselves white knuckling life, or we're too focused on *how* or *when* something will manifest, or who it involves, it limits us and doesn't allow room for life to open the door to even better possibilities.

Anything really is possible in life, and there's always a way (or two or three!) to reach those things you want. So let go a little, surrender and let life guide you.

"Slow down and enjoy life. It's not only the scenery you miss by going too fast – you also miss the sense of where you are going and why."
- Eddie Cantor

81.
Slow Down and Savor the Moments

When we spend our days in a busy blur it's easy for life to feel like a treadmill that you are just running on, without much thought as to where you're going, or if you even want to head in that direction.

When we fly through the day in hustle mode, by the time we hit the pillow at night we can barely remember what we did. Not to mention if we had any fun.

Slow down the pace of your life and start savoring the moments. Eat more leisurely, breathe deeper, laugh longer, drive slower and give your attention to one task at a time.

Take in the people and scenery around you.

Let your body relax and give your mind the space it needs to process things and get creative.

Be more present with the people around you and take time to truly connect.

The best of life is found in the special moments. Slow down the speed of your life and enjoy each one to the fullest.

"Each person deserves a day away in which no problems are confronted, no solutions searched for. Each of us needs to withdraw from the cares which will not withdraw from us."
- Maya Angelou

82.
Take Vacations

Vacations are healthy for your body, mind and soul. Breaking routine and getting a change of scenery spices up our lives. Not to mention, vacations give us the chance to explore the world, appreciate other ways of living and remind us that there's so much more to life than work and chores.

While jobs are necessary to pay the bills, and there's nothing wrong with being dedicated to your career, too often we prioritize the 9-5 grind over relaxing and having fun. But taking time off helps us feel more inspired and allows us to clear our heads and gain perspective. It also lets our bodies de-stress, restore and recharge.

Prioritize vacations and create room in your budget for this crucial line item (and if money is too tight, there are always staycations).

Then, when you're on holiday, read books on the beach, snorkel with colorful fish, climb a mountain or stroll through a museum. Make special memories with your family and friends and with your wonderful self. Gift yourself this much-deserved time to unwind and truly enjoy your life.

Just be sure your vacation isn't so crammed with activities that you don't have time to rest. Or you'll arrive home feeling like you need a vacation from your vacation!

83.
Find Your Happy Place and Go There Often

We all have places that light us up and bring out the best in us. These towns, cities, beaches, mountains, deserts or lakes call to us and make our souls happy. Often from the first time we step foot in these Happy Places we feel a sense of belonging – like we're being welcomed home.

Like with special friends and loved ones, Happy Places lift our spirits and calm our nerves. For good reasons, or for no reason at all, we feel more alive when we are there. Your Happy Place may change in different life seasons and as you change, but the joy and connection felt on a cellular level is always the same.

When you find yourself in a place that makes you come alive and brings a special smile to your face, go there, stay there and return as often as you can. Happy Places bring out the best in us and make us feel like all is right in the world.

*"Don't worry about a thing,
every little thing's gonna be alright."*
- Bob Marley

84.
Release Your Worries

We humans worry a lot. We worry that things we *want* to happen won't. We worry that things we *don't want* to happen will. When we worry in our minds, our bodies feel it too. It wreaks havoc on our nervous systems, disrupts our sleep, and is overall unhealthy and no fun.

Worrying comes in different packages. There are little worries like, "Will I be late for my appointment or miss my flight?" That may seem like a big deal in the moment, but they're nothing in the grand scheme of life. There's worry rooted in stress and overwhelm, like, "How will I complete this enormous project and get dinner ready on time?" Finally, there's the worst of worries concerning health, shelter and survival, like, "Where will I live?" "What's going on with my body?" and "How will I be able to make rent or feed my family?"

You most likely won't escape worries completely, but here are a few things you can do to get some much-deserved relief:

Focus on solutions

All worrying feels bad and is unproductive, but you can combat it by being more solution-oriented. Instead of going round and round lamenting the problem, ponder possibilities and intend for solutions. Taking time to consider situations, make plans, organize, simplify or strategize can be highly productive and beneficial – but worrying for the sake of worrying gets us nowhere.

Consider positive outcomes

You may know the expression, "Worrying is like praying for something you don't want." What we give our attention to grows. That's why it's important to keep your focus on what you *do want* to happen, not what you don't.

Instead of pondering "What ifs?" that don't include happy endings, take a red pen to those endings and make them positive. Stop worrying about the worst thing that can happen and start considering the best thing that can happen.

Cross bridges *IF* you come to them

The great Chinese philosopher Lao Tzu said, "If you are depressed, you are living in the past. If you are anxious, you are living in the future. If you are at peace, you are living in the present."

Many of our worries are about the future and aren't even guaranteed to happen. Stay focused on "the now" and remind yourself, "I can cross that bridge *if* I come to it."

Get support

You are never alone in life. If you feel overly stressed, anxious or worried, reach out and get support from a friend, family member, financial planner, or a life coach to help you organize and create a plan. Meditation classes can do wonders to quiet and calm your mind. Therapists, psychologists, doctors or specialists can be just what you need to unpack, process and work through worries, too. Pay attention to how you feel and don't hesitate to reach out for help.

Build your trust in life

People who are prone to worrying have often lost their trust in life. Perhaps you experienced a trauma or event where you were disappointed or betrayed. This can make you feel like you have to be in control of everything – which isn't possible.

To help you worry less, start rebuilding your trust in life. Jog your memory for those times that you were worried but everything worked out OK. Take note of how life has taken care of you. Set an intention to believe the universe is benevolent and remind yourself what author and speaker Louise Hay always said:

"I am safe. All is well."

Sometimes we worry out of habit, and when we really think about it, if many of our worries came true it wouldn't be the end of the world. Pay attention to your attention and do what you can to lighten your worries and help yourself feel better.

Emily Florence

> Stop worrying about the worst thing that can happen and start considering the **best** thing that can happen.

"Getting over a painful experience is much like crossing monkey bars. You have to let go at some point in order to move forward."
- C.S. Lewis

85.
Forgive and Move Forward

People often think forgiving is an offer of kindness to someone who at one point hurt or wronged us. But we forgive in order to help ourselves. We forgive because holding on to hurt, anger and resentment isn't good for us mentally or physically. We forgive because we were hurt once, and there is no need to give anyone the power to continue doing so by keeping our wounds open. We forgive so that we can finally let go and move forward with our lives.

Forgiving is easier said than done. It's a process and can take time. It's not uncommon to think that in order to forgive, you need to receive an apology or an explanation, but we don't need anything from anyone else in order to forgive. All we need is to have enough love for ourselves to decide we're not going to continue holding on to what's eating away at us. Though our feelings are reasonable, it's not worth letting them linger. As the saying goes, "Resentment is like drinking poison and expecting it to kill your enemy." The only person you harm by holding tight to past anger and hurt is yourself.

You may worry that forgiving means you accept or condone a person's behavior, or that you're opening the door to having them in your life. But forgiving doesn't have to mean any of that. It can purely be an act of self-love.

When you are ready to forgive, you may find working with a therapist to be highly beneficial. Journaling and writing letters with no intention of sending them can also be cathartic, as well as talking openly with trusted friends, or being part of support groups. Even setting the intention to forgive is powerful.

Depending on your circumstances, you may try to understand where the person who you want to forgive was coming from, or to recognize that even though they hurt you, it wasn't their plan. Sometimes forgiveness happens naturally when you find yourself in the other person's shoes and you see everything from a different perspective.

Self-forgiveness is just as important as forgiving others. If you feel regret or even self-hatred for something you did long ago, it's time to make peace with your past. We all make mistakes and learn as we grow. Take a moment to acknowledge what you've done, learn what you can from it, and make amends. If you know you've wronged someone, reach out and apologize, or send them good prayers and blessings. It's never too late to make things right.

Forgiveness can take time, so be patient and go easy. Keep in mind the reason you're doing it in the first place, because holding on to anger, resentment, or pain isn't healthy for you, and it sabotages your happiness. When you finally let go of what's been weighing you down, you'll feel the peace you've been longing for and that you truly deserve.

86.
Flip the Script on Your Life Stories

You may know the saying, *"It's not what happens in life, but how you respond that makes all the difference."* There's a lot of truth to this, and we can either be a constant victim in life, or we can flip the script and be our own superhero.

When something happens, like a job loss or breakup, instead of seeing it as a sad or scary time, you can tell a better story and reframe it in a positive light by viewing it as exciting – a chance for a new beginning and for something even better to happen. At the very least you can see it as an opportunity to learn and grow. After all, making mistakes and getting something wrong helps us to get it right next time.

Uncover the silver linings and highlight the positives. Maybe your marriage blew up, but you are a more honest person because of it. Perhaps the old job was a drain on you, but at least you walked away with friends for life. Maybe you lost a great deal of money, but now you know how to listen to your intuition, and if money came into your life once, it will come again. At the very least, you survived and your past experiences have made you the person you are today.

The stories we tell about our lives tend to play out over and over again, so do your future self a favor and stop identifying with anything you don't want to define you. Don't think or talk about yourself as *always* struggling with money, relationships, jobs, body image, or anything else that you don't want to become an ongoing theme in your life.

Reframe things in a positive light and start telling better stories.

87.
Don't Be Afraid to Choose Again

The beautiful thing about life is we get to start over every day. Anything we don't like about ourselves we can improve. Anything that no longer serves us we can release. It may not be easy, and we may not be able to do it as quickly as we'd like to, but we can take steps now to create a different path for the future.

Some of us perpetuate our own misery by staying stuck, complaining and continuing to create the same unhappy life day after day, telling ourselves we have no choice. The truth is, as long as you're living, breathing and thinking, you can choose to create a better life for yourself.

> The beautiful thing about life is we get to start over every day.

A week before we moved to Hawaii, my pup Harper and I ran into our elderly neighbor Gwennie on a walk. I'd just dropped off my car at the port to ship across the Pacific Ocean and was getting Harper squared away to fly in the airplane cabin with me. (Right next to me in her very own comfort seat!) Having relocated several times from California to the East Coast, moving long-distance wasn't new to me. But moving across an ocean came with a whole host of unfamiliar hurdles. There were several moving pieces, plus, entering the state of Hawaii is a big process for animals since it's a rabies-free state, so extra tests and paperwork must be done for them to avoid quarantine. As Gwennie crouched down to pet Harper, I shared with her all that was on my plate and how much time, energy and organizing was going into the move.

"It's coming together nicely," I told Gwennie as Harper smothered her in kisses and tail wags. "But even with help from my love, family and friends, it's still so much work! What if we don't end up wanting to live there forever?"

Gwennie put her hand on my shoulder, and with her big, blue 87-year-old eyes, she looked at me and said, "Well, Emily, then you guys will just choose something else. Not everything you do has to be forever. It's just life!"

Gwennie smiled and just like that all of the overwhelm I'd felt that day dissipated. *It's just life.*

It may not be easy or possible in the timeline we want it to happen, but when we find ourselves in life patterns or circumstances we've outgrown or that don't make us happy, we really can choose again. It could be a place you call home, or a profession, circle of friends or way of life. Even if it seems impossible, or you'll have to be patient for a while, you can put wheels in motion for anything in your life to change when you decide to. At the very least, you can make the best of your current situation, find more to appreciate, and create a more positive mindset in the meantime.

Like Dolly Parton said, "If you don't like the path you're walking, start paving another one."

88.
Remind Yourself, Tomorrow Is a New Day

We all have those "glass half empty" days when your thoughts lean negative and everything feels like it's just too much. Perhaps you didn't sleep well the night before, or your hormones are a little out of whack. Maybe you're under the weather, or the stars simply aren't on your side.

When we're in these places, it's easy to feel overwhelmed, or like we're failing at life. It's easy to turn molehills into mountains and get tangled up in thinking the worst.

These days can trick you, so be aware of your moods, and when you're experiencing an off day, go easy. Don't overthink anything or make big life decisions. Don't do anything rash or say something you may regret. If you're feeling especially low, seek help – you are never alone.

Take things one moment at a time and get back to basics. Dedicate the day to your mental, physical and spiritual well-being. Eat well, rest and hydrate.

The older we get the easier it is to recognize our moods and to try not to take them so seriously. Just like the sky looks different at sunrise than it does midday, sometimes all we need is a talk with a friend, a good night's rest and a fresh new morning to see things in a different light. Tides turn quickly and wash away low moods, so whatever has you feeling ready to throw in the towel now may look entirely different by daybreak.

Go easy on low-feeling days, and remember, this isn't the rest of your life. Trite but true, this too shall pass and tomorrow is a brand-new day.

89.
Let the Little Things Go

There's a lot to be upset about at times. There's also quite a bit that gets under our skin and throws us off course that doesn't deserve the attention we give it.

What we give our attention to grows. When we think about, talk about and obsess about something that upsets us, it only fuels the fire. While there's no need to bury things in life, we don't need to create big deals out of anything that truly doesn't need to be one. Life is a lot more fun when we let the little things go!

In the bestselling book *Don't Sweat the Small Stuff and It's All Small Stuff,* author Dr. Richard Carlson tells readers when something's upsetting them to ask themselves if it will matter one year from now. It's a simple question that provides so much perspective.

He then says, if the answer is "yes," to go ahead and feel it and deal with it. But if the answer is "no" or "probably not," then take a deep breath and let it go.

Little upsets happen to all of us, but don't let them ruin your day by giving them oxygen. Things burnout much quicker when you don't stoke the fire, so process it out loud to yourself for a few minutes or call a friend if you need to vent, then drop it and move on. Resist carrying something around all day and talking to everyone you encounter about it, or posting on social media where comments will keep it alive for days. There's no need to let that driver who cut you off Friday morning still upset you on a beautiful Sunday afternoon.

"Life moves pretty fast. If you don't stop and look around once in a while you could miss it."
- Ferris Bueller

90.
Take Inventory of Your Life

Weeks go slow, but years fly by. It's easy to get so caught up in the day-to-day that we lose sight of the direction we want to be heading and all that we're accomplishing along the way. That's why every now and then we need to take a pause to check in on our lives and take inventory.

Taking Inventory is a simple exercise to help you connect with your life, recognize where you are and get clear on where you'd like to go next. And all it takes is a pen, paper and 30 minutes of uninterrupted time.

It's important to note how common it is to feel that accomplishments are reserved for major life events like buying a house, reaching a money goal, running a marathon or writing a book. But often, it's the dark days, difficult times and hard-learned lessons that deserve recognition in order to propel us into the next chapter of our lives.

Schedule time for yourself to pour a cup of coffee or a glass of something that makes you happy and take inventory of your life. Congratulate yourself on all that you've achieved, get clear on what you'd like to experience next and remember what you're really living for.

Taking inventory exercise

- What life changes have occurred in the past year? (Did you move, change your career, adjust your lifestyle, start a family, fall in love, end an unhealthy relationship, start a business, buy or sell a house, etc.?)
- Did you have any adventures? Where did you go, what did you do and see?
- Who's come into your life recently? Who's left? (Friends, neighbors, partners, co-workers, pets, etc.)
- What was your absolute high of the past year? What was your low?
- How have you grown lately? What life lessons, trades or skills have you learned?
- What does your income, savings and overall money situation look like right now?
- What would you like your finances to look like one year from now?
- What health or self-care improvements have you made to your lifestyle? (Walking, meditation, better food choices, etc.)
- What are you most proud of yourself for right now?

- What was the most fun or romantic moment you experienced recently?
- What are you ready to release from your life? How can you find more peace?
- What do you want your life to look like one year from now? In three years? In five years?
- What word best describes your life right now? (Blessed, Peaceful, Changing, Chaotic, Challenging, Happy, Abundant, etc.)

"Love yourself first and everything else falls into line. You really have to love yourself to get anything done in this world."
- Lucille Ball

91.
Love Yourself More

When my niece Emery was 6 months old and crawling wildly, she discovered her reflection in the full-length mirror. Each time she saw herself, she'd light up with a smile, crawl over to the mirror, lean in, and give herself a great big kiss!

We should all look in the mirror and, at the very least, give ourselves a smile. Life can deal us bad hands and we need to keep our confidence cup brimming, champion ourselves often and loudly, and care for ourselves like it's our number one job.

Watch your words and listen to how you speak to yourself. When you notice you are being hard on yourself ask yourself, "Would I say this to a friend?" If the answer is "No" then rephrase it in a more supportive way. Negative self-talk tugs at our self-esteem and over time, all of the seemingly harmless self-deprecating jokes take a toll, and our confidence plummets. Like a loose thread on a favorite sweater, if we ignore the small damage we're inflicting, it grows until one day we wake up to find a gaping hole in our self-esteem.

If your confidence is on shaky ground, place a picture of yourself as a child on your bathroom mirror and make a promise to give him or her the very best care you can. When you feel like you're about to go into self-blame, put yourself down, or let someone take advantage of you, take a look at the innocent, wide-eyed, wonderful you as a child, and vow to take a stand for yourself.

Life can be a wild ride, and the more love you have for yourself, the more comforted you'll feel knowing there's always someone on your team - *you*. So take a cue from my niece Emery and give a big ole' kiss to that wonderful person staring back in the mirror!

You are the storyteller of your life. Remember to love the main character.

92.
Accept Compliments

It's easy to give out compliments, but when it comes to being on the receiving end, most of us deflect or downplay them and don't fully take them in.

Does any of this sound familiar?

Friend: "Is that a new sweater? That's such a great color on you!"

You: "Oh this old thing?"

Friend: "Your salad dressing tastes amazing!"

You: "You think? I thought it was a little too sweet."

Friend: "Congratulations on your big promotion!"

You: "Haha, thanks. I think I only got it because there was no one else left to promote."

Modesty and humility are wonderful characteristics, but when someone offers you a compliment it's important to let it sink in. It's love coming your way, so resist brushing it off and instead just say, "Thank you."

Take note of how good the kudos made you feel and keep the compliment ball rolling by paying one forward. It could make someone else's day!

93.
Highlight the Good

It's important to end the day feeling good, but when our days whiz by without any reflection, we often hit the pillow recalling the hiccups or feeling like we barely scratched the surface of what we set out to do. We forget all of the amazing things we accomplished and the good fortune we experienced, and without meaning to, we become hard on ourselves and down on our lives.

Shine a spotlight on all of the good you experience each day by taking a few minutes before bedtime to reflect. Think of the accomplishments and everything that went well in your day. Did you make a green light? Feel a genuine smile on your face when talking with a neighbor? Take a small step toward a goal? Write them down or list them in your head while brushing your teeth.

Even the tiniest wins deserve recognition. If you're a new parent, taking a shower may be the only thing you were able to accomplish that day – and good for you!

Recognize everything you tackle each day and all of the blessings you experience. Shine a spotlight on the good and let anything negative fade into the background.

94.
Keep in Mind, We're All Going Through Something

Every person we encounter has something going on in their lives that we don't know about. We don't walk around holding signs sharing what's going on deep down, so it's easy to forget that people have struggles beyond what we can see.

It's good to keep this in mind when your server gives you the wrong change, your neighbor doesn't call you back right away and your loved one is uncharacteristically short with you. You don't know if she's waiting on a call from a doctor and is worried and fragile. You don't know if his wife is dealing with postpartum depression and he's sleep deprived and afraid. You don't know if they had a hard day at work or school and someone treated them unfairly.

You never need to excuse or ignore a person's bad behavior, but it's good to be mindful of a bigger picture. Since we rarely share our innermost fears and pain with just anyone, sometimes not even those people we love the most, we never fully know what another human being is going through – as much as we may want to.

Throughout the day try your best to:

Give people a break.

Give people the benefit of the doubt.

Be patient.

Be understanding.

Be compassionate.

We may not know what someone is going through, but keep in mind we are all going through something.

"You can tell a lot about a person by the way they handle three things: a rainy day, lost luggage and tangled Christmas tree lights."

- Maya Angelou

95.
Stay Calm and Holiday On

From stringing lights to wrapping gifts, the most wonderful time of the year often comes with a side of hectic. Though the holiday season overflows with merriment, on any given day joy and melancholy can be intertwined like twinkly lights wrapped 'round a tree. We cry happy tears hugging loved ones we are blessed to be near, and wipe away tears of sorrow missing those who are no longer by our side. Then there's all the cooking, traveling, and decorating that can cause our heads to spin.

If you find yourself caught up scrambling to find the perfect gifts, or losing sight of all the love, joy and good cheer that the season is truly about, here are a few ways to help keep the "happy" in your holidays:

Count your blessings

Gifts may need to be wrapped and cards mailed, but nothing is as important during the holiday season as taking time to recognize how much you have to be thankful for. Instead of making lists of more things you need to do, make lists of everything you have to be grateful for. Even if your flight's delayed or your over-the-top aunt is going on a political rant, keep in mind all of the food, friends and family you are truly blessed with.

Give freely

The holidays are a time of giving, so lend a helping hand to friends, neighbors, people and animals in your community. Volunteer at a local shelter, or spend an afternoon nibbling cookies with a neighbor who lives alone. Give clothing, shoes, blankets and towels to local homeless and animal shelters. Give toys to kids who could use some good cheer. Give smiles, hugs and love to everyone around you.

Take time alone

Calendars tend to get crammed during the holidays and it's important to take time to yourself. Even a 10-minute walk in nature or a free write in your journal can do wonders to clear your head and ground you. Gift yourself this time alone so you can show up as your best self for your loved ones and at all of those holiday gatherings.

Get swept up in the spirit of the season

Take a cue from children and allow yourself to feel the excitement, joy, and wonder surrounding the holidays. Cozy up by a fire with a cup of hot cocoa. Savor the smell of Christmas trees and the sight of twinkling lights. Sing out loud, throw snowballs, play a game of dreidel, and let yourself be swept up by the magic, remembering – 'tis the season to be jolly.

The holiday season is a magical time of year. Be merry and bright and savor the special moments. Like a snowflake in all its unique beauty, it'll be gone too soon.

"Life is like riding a bicycle. To keep your balance, you must keep moving."
- Albert Einstein

96.
Keep Going, Keep Growing

Life is full of detours and delays. Most likely there will be times when you feel like you've raced up the mountain, then somehow fell off track. You may even get down on yourself for moving slower than expected on something you set out to accomplish, and be tempted to throw in the towel.

We can't always move full steam ahead and not every day will be smooth sailing. Often, we make big leaps, then tumble back a step – and pausing to rest is necessary. It's part of the process of improving ourselves and going for our dreams. We learn and grow, and very often we re-learn and grow more.

Dr. Martin Luther King, Jr. said, "If you can't fly then run, if you can't run then walk, if you can't walk then crawl, but whatever you do, you have to keep moving forward."

Walk your life path with your head held high and your belief in yourself strong. Take breaks when you need to recharge, but stay optimistic and tenacious in your pursuit. And on those days when you feel like you are stuck or even moving backward, remind yourself it's all a part of the process.

When you follow what sparks fire in your soul, you feel happy and fulfilled. And as long as you keep moving forward on your life dreams, you are in fact progressing – even when it doesn't feel like it.

Remember, small steps lead to great gains, and good things really do take time.

"I've learned that people will forget what you said, people will forget what you did, but people will never forget how you made them feel."
- Maya Angelou

97.
Treasure Your Friends and Family

We all know what matters most in life: The people we love and those who love us back.

Though we don't mean to, we can get so caught up in the daily grind or our never-ending to-dos, that we can forget to tell those people who mean so much to us that we really, truly care. We might even take for granted the people who we appreciate most. That's why it's important to prioritize your closest relationships and take time to connect with people who add meaning and love to your life.

Make showing up for your friends and family a priority in your day. Take time to ask them how they are *really* doing and let them know how much they mean to you. Show up for them in person as often as you can and give them thanks for making your life all that it is.

While personal achievements are to be celebrated, the biggest accomplishments in life are the relationships we keep. At the end of the day, it's the people we love and who love us back that make all of the difference in our lives.

"You begin by always expecting good things to happen."
- Tom Hopkins

98.
Always Be Ready to Celebrate

Growing up, our family fridge was never without a bottle of Champagne. The bubbly goodness isn't a daily delight for our family – simple wine is more our style – but Champagne is our go-to for celebrating, and our fridge was always in supply.

One day I asked my dad about it and he smiled and said, "Emily, a home should always be ready to welcome good news and a reason to celebrate!"

My brother and I hit the jackpot with our parents, and have been lucky to receive so much wisdom throughout the years, but this little nugget has always been a favorite of mine.

Great news arrives in every home in the form of promotions, engagements, babies, goals achieved, awards won, milestones reached, and fears overcome. Whether it's a bottle of Champagne, Prosecco or sparkling water, try adding some bubbly goodness to your fridge as a reminder to expect a reason to celebrate. Just seeing the bottle when you open the door will serve as a reminder that soon you'll be popping it open and clinking a glass in cheers.

Life is full of wonderful surprises. Always be ready to welcome good news and a reason to celebrate.

> Life is full of wonderful surprises. Always be ready to welcome good news and a reason to celebrate.

99.
Enjoy Your Life More

Most people don't look back on life thinking, "I wish I didn't have so much fun!" More often, it's thoughts like, "Why did I take things so seriously? Why did I get caught up in dramas that didn't really matter? Why didn't I take more time off for family and friends and to enjoy myself more?" that fills our minds.

Life is meant to be enjoyed. While work may be necessary, many of us feel we have to earn the chance to enjoy ourselves. That enjoyment can come *only after* everything else is taken care of. Some people even feel guilty if they sit down with a book or head out for a mid-day walk when there's still work and to-dos to be done.

Sometimes, we overload ourselves and only allow ourselves a break when we're sick. This begs the question: Would we be sick if we had allowed ourselves to rest? Do we sometimes feel that being under the weather is the only way to give ourselves permission to lay around and do nothing – guilt free?

Enjoyment is our birthright and taking time to relax, have fun and do a whole lotta nothing isn't something you need to earn. There's no need to reward yourself with it on a weekend *only after* running yourself ragged during the weekdays. Nor does relaxing have to be scheduled into your calendar for months down the road when you'll be vacationing in Tahiti – or years later when you'll be retired. You deserve to enjoy life's simple pleasures right now.

Take time each day to kick back and enjoy yourself. Lounge by a pool, snuggle up and read a feel-good book, laugh over lunch with friends, and play so much with your kids and pets that you lose track of time.

Life is precious, and it goes by fast. Enjoy it as much as you can – while you can.

"Not all of us can do great things. But we can do small things with great love."
- Mother Theresa

100.
Spread Joy

We are far more powerful than we give ourselves credit for, and each of us can make a positive difference in another person's life every single day. The good news is you don't have to break the bank, skimp on sleep or spend hours of time to do plenty of good.

The happier everyone else is, the happier you will be too, so make it a point each day to be a bright spot for someone and spread joy:

- Be the first to wave, smile and say, "Good morning."
- Give out compliments.
- Pay for the person's coffee in line behind you.
- Drop spare change into someone's parking meter that's close to expiring.
- Pick a bouquet of flowers for residents at a nearby nursing home to enjoy.

- Gather old towels and blankets to give to animal shelters or your local Humane Society.
- Bake or buy cookies for your neighbors, or invite them over for tea (especially if they live alone).
- Send a text to a friend or family member and tell them you're thinking about them and you are grateful they're in your life.
- Start a toy drive at your office for kids in need. Set out a box and email your coworkers, inviting them to take part. Then, deliver the gifts to a nearby shelter.
- Be a more relaxed driver and give the car in front of you extra room.
- Offer your seat on the subway to someone who looks like they could use a break.
- Be mindful about what you share on social media and make your posts uplifting.
- Tell one person what a great job they're doing and how much you appreciate them.
- Take time to really listen when someone is talking to you.
- Go easier on yourself. All love begins with self-love and the kinder you are to yourself, the kinder you will be to others.

We are all in this life together and we need to take care of one another. Little loving gestures go a long way, and kindness is contagious. Make it a point to bring more light into this world and create a positive ripple effect. Author Alice Morse Earle once said, "Every day may not be good, but there's something good in every day."

Be that something good for someone today.

101.
Trust Something Even Better Is in Store

On the eve of my birthday, I go somewhere peaceful to watch the sunset and take a moment to say goodbye to the past year. The location changes from year to year, but I always make sure to capture the moment with a photo.

A few years back, I chose a favorite lookout spot of mine surrounded by mountains. I parked my car and started making my way by foot down the dirt path. The mountains were still, and big golden fluffy clouds floated all the way out to the ocean. With each step my heart lit up – it was going to be a spectacular sunset.

I climbed on top of a large rock and smiled as the mountains prepared to dazzle me with their ever-enchanting pink moment – a magical few minutes where the mountains glow a vibrant magenta and then quietly fade to a soft tranquil blush. The moment is so spectacular it can take your breath away.

I pulled my phone from my coat pocket eager to capture this beautiful display of nature, and felt the smile on my face fall. My phone was frozen.

Nature doesn't pause for any of us, and as the colors continued to charm, I frantically powered the device on and off, but nothing worked. My phone had been taken captive by evil technology gremlins and there was nothing I could do.

After a few more frustrating attempts to revive my phone, I finally surrendered, snapping a picture of the fantastic sunset in my head.

I stayed on that rock for a while after the sun fell, soaking up every bit of the now soft pink, violet and golden clouds. Then as dark began creeping in, I started the short walk along the dirt path to my car. As I neared the parking lot, I came upon a couple who were packing up fancy camera gear. They were photographers.

As we said "hello" and "good evening" to one another, I shared with them my birthday tradition and asked if they got any good shots that I could purchase.

"Tons!" The man replied.

"What a sunset!" the woman exclaimed.

And with a quick exchange of our email addresses, they promised to send me a few of their photos. "No charge!" they said. "It's our pleasure."

Fifteen minutes later, I pulled into my driveway and my phone lit up. Without doing a thing, it was suddenly back to its healthy self. And a few minutes later a sweet "Happy Birthday" email came in from the photographers. Attached to it was a spectacular photo of me sitting on top of the rock, staring out to the golden sky, surrounded by pink mountains and purple clouds, just as the sun was setting on the eve of my birthday. It was the most beautiful photo I'd ever seen of a sunset and to this day one of my most cherished pictures.

I sat in my car a few minutes longer, staring in awe at the photo, and I couldn't help but laugh. I had been devastated when my phone froze, fearing I wouldn't be able to capture the moment, and now here was this picture more incredible than anything I could've taken myself.

This story of how my phone going temporarily mad ultimately led to me receiving one of my favorite photos of all time isn't a big deal in the grand scheme of things. But many other big life moments that initially felt like a calamity or devastation ended up opening the door for something even better to come into my life. Like when a cancelled flight plus a 3-day travel delay led me to meet one of my favorite friends on the planet. Or when the owners of a house I didn't particularly love backed out of renting it to me, and it led to me moving into my dream home a week later. Even a heartbreaking loss opened space in my heart to welcome in one of the greatest loves of my life.

In his 2005 Stanford University Commencement speech, Steve Jobs said, *"You can't connect the dots looking forward; you can only connect them looking backward. So, you have to trust that the dots will somehow connect in your future. You have to trust in something – your gut, destiny, life, karma, whatever. Because believing that the dots will connect down the road will give you the confidence to follow your heart even when it leads you off the well-worn path – and that will make all the difference."*

The course of life doesn't always go as planned. The dreams and wishes we hold don't always manifest or come to fruition as we want them to. We face challenges we never saw coming and setbacks we never expected or deserved. Having faith isn't always easy. When things aren't going your way, it can be easier to feel that life is out to get you. That job you lost, the person who didn't want to be with you, the house that passed on your offer – all of these disappointments may temporarily rob you of your belief in yourself or your trust in life to deliver. But like Steve Jobs said to those eager graduates, so often it's *only* when we're looking backward that we see how life was unfolding in our favor, though it didn't feel like it at the time. If we are lucky, we see a silver lining quickly, but sometimes it takes months or years to realize something we once considered a loss, unwanted or unfair, was actually a gift.

Life won't always go how we want it to, and the universe works in mysterious ways. We can feel like things aren't working in our favor, but so often we just can't see the whole picture yet. Every rejection truly *is* redirection, and blessings often lie waiting in disguise. Instead of seeing something as happening against you, start looking at it as the door cracking open for something *even better* to happen for you. Have faith that life is rearranging itself in your favor and that someday it will all make sense. Looking back, it always does.

Remember, not every storm that enters your life is meant to bring you down. Most come to clear the way. And you know what they say always comes after the rain.

> *"Tell me, what is it you plan to do with your one wild and precious life?"*
> - Mary Oliver

Dear Reader

Life can be challenging, messy, and downright hard. But when we look for it, there's so much we can find to be thankful for right now, and so much we can do to create more happiness, love, calm, and ease in our days – no matter what's going on around us. I hope this book helps guide you.

In many ways, life is yours to choose. So ask yourself:

What is it that I truly want for my life?

What do I want to experience?

Where do I want to go?

What do I want to see?

Who do I want to spend my time with?

What kind of person do I want to be?

Writer Joseph Campbell said, "As you go the way of life, you will see a great chasm. Jump. It is not as wide as you think." You are stronger and more capable than you may even know. Don't ever doubt the power you have to create a life that's even better.

Decide what you want for your life, what you don't, and...

Choose it.

Own it.

Love it.

Go on and live it.

Thank you for reading.

Sign up for my newsletter for more.

www.EmilyFlorence.com

Acknowledgements

My biggest thanks and huge hugs to everyone who contributed to this project in great, big and tiny, small ways – this book wouldn't be what it is without you.

Also, my greatest appreciation to my editors and book team for your brilliance and dedication to making this book even better. Leslie Barrie Loh, you've been on this journey with me from the beginning through rounds of edits, hours of phone calls and going back and forth over one-liners. Thank you for your patience and enthusiasm every time I said, "That's a wrap!" and then came back with another idea. You are an exceptional editor and hands-down one of the loveliest people I've ever met. Delilah De La Rosa you've been my friend and editor and someone who has inspired me in life for over two decades (with many more to come!). Thank you for shining your incredible wisdom and light onto the pages and for guiding the book to its best flow. Your support and encouragement meant everything and it's been a blast to be on this journey with you. Sarah Carrillo Riswick, I've been honored to collaborate with you on many wonderful projects and it's been a joy to get to join forces on this project with you too. You are a fantastic editor and I thank you for your practical and thoughtful guidance and for always knowing how to make a sentence shine. This book's been surrounded by the most amazing people, and I'm thankful for the entire team and everyone involved with Good Day Publishing.

My life wouldn't be what it is if not for the wonderful people in it. My biggest thanks to my parents, Susan and Jim Florence and to my brother, Brent, who have shaped my life in so many incredible ways. Thank you for your love and support and for always encouraging me to do work that is meaningful and to believe in myself – even when it's hard.

A big, huge thanks to so many more people I'm lucky to have in my corner and who have supported me. A special shout-out to Natalie Gelman, Mary Squellati, Suzanne Duca, Jessa and the Brooks family, the Squellati family, the Spaccarotelli family, Reece Duca, Tom Faia, Rachel Powell, David Bluestone, Tony C., Lisa B., Jess G., Grant H. and Dave O.

Being in the writing cave can get lonely, but I was lucky to never feel alone thanks to my dog, Harper. Harper, thank you for being the sweetest and silliest pup on the planet and for always smiling and wagging your tail to encourage me – even when my desk light woke you up at 5 a.m. for early morning writing sessions. There's a saying, "Whoever said diamonds are a girl's best friend never had a dog," and I couldn't agree more!

Last, but certainly not least, I want to thank you, dear reader, for going on this journey with me. Each time I sat down to write I intended for at least one thing in this book to be of value to you. I hope this book serves as inspiration and encouragement and that you're able to take away a lesson or story that will make a positive difference in your life.

No person is an island, and neither is the creation of a book. Thank you all!

About Emily Florence

Emily Florence is an award-winning writer, journalist and certified life, life purpose and career coach. She has been featured in major media outlets including *Forbes, Entrepreneur, The Huffington Post* and the *Los Angeles Business Journal*.

Emily has a Master of Arts degree in Broadcast Journalism from Emerson College in Boston and a Bachelor of Arts degree in Cultural Anthropology from the University of California at Santa Barbara. Her first company was named a *Forbes Top 100 Website for Women* and a *w3 Award Winner for Best Writing for a Lifestyle Website*.

Emily spends her time between a town in California and an island in the state of Hawaii with her family and her dog, Harper.

Learn more and sign up for her newsletter at
www.EmilyFlorence.com.

*"Your heart knows the way.
Run in that direction."*
- Rumi

www.ingramcontent.com/pod-product-compliance
Lightning Source LLC
Chambersburg PA
CBHW020418010526
44118CB00010B/315